**New Directions for
Institutional Research**

Paul D. Umbach
EDITOR-IN-CHIEF

J. Fredericks Volkwein
ASSOCIATE EDITOR

Assessing Complex General Education Student Learning Outcomes

Jeremy D. Penn
EDITOR

Number 149 • Spring 2011
Jossey-Bass
San Francisco

ASSESSING COMPLEX GENERAL EDUCATION STUDENT LEARNING OUTCOMES
Jeremy D. Penn (ed.)
New Directions for Institutional Research, no. 149
Paul D. Umbach, Editor-in-Chief

NEW DIRECTIONS FOR INSTITUTIONAL RESEARCH (ISSN 0271-0579, electronic ISSN 1536-075X) is part of The Jossey-Bass Higher and Adult Education Series and is published quarterly by Wiley Subscription Services, Inc., A Wiley Company, at Jossey-Bass, 989 Market Street, San Francisco, California 94103-1741 (publication number USPS 098-830). Periodicals Postage Paid at San Francisco, California, and at additional mailing offices. POSTMASTER: Send address changes to New Directions for Institutional Research, Jossey-Bass, 989 Market Street, San Francisco, California 94103-1741.

SUBSCRIPTIONS cost $109 for individuals and $280 for institutions, agencies, and libraries in the United States. See order form at end of book.

EDITORIAL CORRESPONDENCE should be sent to Paul D. Umbach, Leadership, Policy and Adult and Higher Education, North Carolina State University, Poe 300, Box 7801, Raleigh, NC 27695-7801.

New Directions for Institutional Research is indexed in *Academic Search* (EBSCO), *Academic Search Elite* (EBSCO), *Academic Search Premier* (EBSCO), *CIJE: Current Index to Journals in Education* (ERIC), *Contents Pages in Education* (T&F), *Current Abstracts* (EBSCO), *EBSCO Professional Development Collection* (EBSCO), *Educational Research Abstracts Online* (T&F), *ERIC Database* (Education Resources Information Center), *Higher Education Abstracts* (Claremont Graduate University), *Multicultural Education Abstracts* (T&F), *Sociology of Education Abstracts* (T&F).

Microfilm copies of issues and chapters are available in 16mm and 35mm, as well as microfiche in 105mm, through University Microfilms, Inc., 300 North Zeeb Road, Ann Arbor, Michigan 48106-1346.

www.josseybass.com

Contents

Editor's Notes

Marc Chun (2002) tells a joke about a young boy who happened upon a man who was crawling around on his hands and knees under a streetlight.

> The boy stopped the man and asked, "What are you doing?"
> "I'm looking for my wallet," the man replied, turning back to his search.
> "I'll help you look," the boy exclaimed. "Where did you lose it?"
> The man pointed to the end of the block, near a large, dark oak tree. "Somewhere near that tree."
> Puzzled, the boy asked, "Then why are you looking over here?"
> The man looked up at the boy. "The light's better here."

Too often, our work at assessing student learning in higher education is like the man's experience in the story: we choose what to assess on the basis of what we think is easiest to measure, or worse yet on the assessment instruments that we happen to have at hand or that are the flavor of the month. As a result, we end up assessing student learning outcomes that are inconsequential and have little impact on our institutional mission, or we resort to assessing "student satisfaction," summarizing student grade point averages, or looking up our ranking in *U.S. News and World Report*. But if we want the considerable time and effort we have invested in assessment to provide meaningful data that can be used to improve our educational programs and lend evidence to external stakeholders that we are meeting our educational goals, then we must move beyond assessment by happenstance or convenience, and work instead to tackle the complex and meaningful student learning outcomes that represent the heart of our institutions' work.

This volume grew out of my frustration at not finding clear and simple guidance on how to assess complex general education student learning outcomes such as critical thinking, teamwork, and civic engagement, and out of a fascinating presentation by Pamela Steinke and Peggy Fitch at the North Carolina State Assessment Symposium, titled "Measuring Complex General Education Outcomes." The purpose of this volume is to give faculty members and assessment leaders the tools and resources needed to engage in the important work of assessing complex general education student learning outcomes.

In conceptualizing this volume, I divided it into two parts. Part One, made up of two chapters, presents a broad overview of the issue. Chapter One builds an argument for assessing general education outcomes and addresses some common critiques of general education assessment work. Chapter Two, as a bridge to Part Two, describes a systematic process, based

New Directions for Institutional Research, no. 149, Spring 2011 © Wiley Periodicals, Inc.
Published online in Wiley Online Library (wileyonlinelibrary.com) • DOI: 10.1002/ir.375

1

on research practices in the field of psychology, to develop assessment measures and processes for assessing complex student learning outcomes.

Part Two presents an in-depth examination of six key complex general education student learning outcomes: critical thinking, quantitative reasoning, teamwork, intercultural competence, civic knowledge and engagement, and integrative and applied learning. In each of these six chapters, the authors define the outcome using a theoretical foundation, highlight practices that have been shown to (or have promise for leading to) student achievement of the outcome, and present guidance on how to select or create assessment measures and processes for gathering evidence on student achievement of the outcome. These chapters can be used to impart momentum in establishing or refining practices for teaching and assessing these six outcomes; or they can be used as outlines for developing a process for assessing other complex student learning outcomes that we were not able to include in this volume.

The volume closes with a forward-looking chapter that proposes direction for additional innovation in the assessment of complex general education student learning outcomes and proposes an agenda for future research in this area.

I am deeply indebted to Pamela Steinke and Peggy Fitch, who stopped work on a similar book to participate in this project. I also offer my gratitude to the authors of the other chapters—Donald Hatcher, who graciously came on at the last minute and filled in; Nathan Grawe; Richard Hughes; Steven Jones; Darla Deardorff; Julie Hatcher; Marcia Mentkowski; and Stephen Sharkey—and to the patient and helpful series editor, Paul Umbach. Finally, to all of the assessment leaders and faculty members who take up this sometimes thankless work, thank you for your efforts to improve our educational programs and for all that you do.

Jeremy D. Penn
Editor

Reference

Chun, M. "Looking Where the Light Is Better: A Review of the Literature on Assessing Higher Education Quality." *Peer Review*, 2002, 4(2/3), 16–25.

JEREMY D. PENN *is the director of assessment and testing and an adjunct faculty member in the School of Educational Studies at Oklahoma State University.*

NEW DIRECTIONS FOR INSTITUTIONAL RESEARCH • DOI: 10.1002/ir

PART ONE

Background and Theory

1

This chapter gives a brief history of general education assessment, responds to common criticisms of general education assessment, and makes a case for assessing general education as a critical element of our responsibility as faculty members.

The Case for Assessing Complex General Education Student Learning Outcomes

Jeremy D. Penn

Evaluation of educational achievement has been a part of education since at least 589–613 A.D. (Pinar, Reynolds, Slattery, and Taubman, 1996). Liberal education, the foundational element for many general education programs, has existed even longer, with Aristotle, Plato, and other Greek philosophers developing its philosophical foundations in the fourth century B.C. (Mulcahy, 2008). The industrial revolution in the nineteenth century in the United States challenged the idea of a liberal education and brought rise to the factory model of schooling, in which students were "processed," separated into "age-related cohorts called classes or standards," and taught "a standard course" through "teacher-centered methods" (Hargreaves, 1994) for the purpose of preparing students for a life of work. Newman (1947), along with other defenders of the traditional view of liberal education, continued to argue for "knowledge which is its own end" (p. 98) and education as "the cultivation of the intellect" (p. 107).

Modern approaches to general education have integrated the traditional view of liberal education with preparation for work into an overall "preparation for life and personal development" (Mulcahy, 2008, p. 177) that includes learning for its own sake and workplace readiness. The National Leadership Council for Liberal Education and America's Promise issued a challenge to all postsecondary institutions to implement a curriculum with a "comprehensive set of aims and outcomes that are essential for all students" (National Leadership Council for Liberal Education and America's Promise, 2007, p. 4), including such outcomes as teamwork, critical thinking, and communication. A large number of higher education

NEW DIRECTIONS FOR INSTITUTIONAL RESEARCH, no. 149, Spring 2011 © Wiley Periodicals, Inc.
Published online in Wiley Online Library (wileyonlinelibrary.com) • DOI: 10.1002/ir.376

institutions in the United States have been responding to the changing conceptions of general education by revising their general education programs (Johnson, Ratcliff, and Gaff, 2004).

Assessment of general education also has a long history, although relative to the age of liberal education and educational evaluation it is a very recent development. One of the first recorded efforts to comprehensively assess student achievement in higher education in the United States occurred in the late 1920s and early 1930s, when many institutions had general education programs in practice but not necessarily in name. In this effort, nearly forty-five thousand high school and college students were given a multiple-choice test that assessed students' knowledge of the physical world, mathematics and science, and the social world including psychology, sociology, statistical methods, and ancient cultures (Learned and Wood, 1938). In an approach that foreshadowed the popularity of value-added methodology, the test was given to a group of students as sophomores and again two years later when they were seniors at forty-five institutions. Learning gains of 0.02 to 0.56 standard deviations were found at the school level and used to rank institutions into achievement groups. The researchers found "there were few 'surprises' in the placement of colleges as determined by their achievement-test averages" (1938, p. 15).

Further solidifying the importance of assessment of educational achievement was Ralph Tyler's book on curriculum development and evaluation. Tyler identified four questions to guide curriculum development and evaluation, focusing on identification of educational purposes, selection and organization of educational experiences, and whether or not those experiences were "actually producing the desired results" (Tyler, 1949, p. 105).

Although students' achievement of general education goals has been assessed since at least the 1930s, use of assessment of general education as an institutional improvement and accountability methodology has its roots in the mid-1980s. In 1984, the Study Group on the Conditions of Excellence in American Higher Education recommended using assessment "as a means to provide information about the teaching and learning process and as feedback to help improve the effectiveness with which students, faculty, and the institution carry out their work" (p. 53). In 1985, the First National Conference on Assessment in Higher Education was held in Columbia, South Carolina—further evidence that the higher education assessment movement was well under way (Ewell, 2002). By 1987, 55 percent of surveyed institutions had established an assessment program, and by 1993 this had increased to 98 percent (Ewell, 2002). All six regional accreditors now require assessment of general education as a condition of accreditation, firmly establishing assessment of general education as a key element of institutional accountability and improvement.

NEW DIRECTIONS FOR INSTITUTIONAL RESEARCH • DOI: 10.1002/ir

Tackling Critiques of Assessment of General Education

The long history of general education assessment includes numerous critiques of general education assessment practices. For instance, more than seventy years ago Learned and Wood (1938) identified concerns "with the extent to which the so-called comprehensive, objective, or 'new-type' tests, less familiar ten years ago than now, would prove to justify their use for the purposes in view" (p. 13). Practices for assessing general education are often critiqued for their philosophical foundations, the quality of assessment measures, the relationship between teaching practices and assessment, and the role of academic freedom and external accountability (see Bresciani, 2007; Ewell, 2002; Hutchings, Marchese, and Wright, 1991; Kramer, 2009).

This section responds to five of the most pervasive critiques.

General Education Learning Outcomes Cannot Be Defined. Schwyzer (2007) summarizes the core of this critique when he writes about education as a transformative experience that can change the direction of students' lives, concluding "there's no [student learning outcome] that can measure that" (para. 13). Developing a definition of a complex learning outcome, a process usually called *construct validation* by researchers, can be challenging. Fortunately, much work in this area has already been completed. (See Chapter Two of this volume for a description of one approach grounded in psychology, and the chapters in Part Two for examples.) For example, Cronbach (1955) suggested a variety of methods to establish construct validity, or to "make clear what something is" (p. 290), including examination of differences between two groups that are expected to differ on the construct (for example, freshmen and seniors), use of correlation matrices and factor analyses across multiple measures of a construct, examination of the internal structure of the test itself, and study of changes in the scores over a number of occasions (see Campbell and Fiske, 1959, for more details). The approaches developed as part of construct validation and described in this volume can be used to define any complex general education student learning outcome.

General Education Learning Outcomes Cannot Be Assessed with Existing Tools. The lack of meaningful measures of student achievement on complex general education outcomes could be due to faculty disagreement on what to measure, by the expense of developing measures, or by resistance on the part of colleges (Hersh, 2005). Faculty disagreement can be addressed by implementing a process to develop a clear, research-based definition (see Chapter Two of this volume) or by implementing a systematic process for building faculty engagement (see Maki, 2004).

Some existing assessment measures are expensive, but there are many that are not, or even free. One source to use in searching for existing tools is the Buros Institute of Mental Measurements (http://www.unl.edu/buros/), which publishes the *Mental Measurements Yearbook* approximately bienni-ally. The yearbook summarizes and critically analyzes hundreds of newly released instruments in every volume. Another source is the *Valid Assessment of Learning in Undergraduate Education* (VALUE) project, which brought together national experts in fifteen areas to develop meta-rubrics (http://www.aacu.org/value/rubrics) that are free for use or adaption. In addition, each chapter in Part Two of this volume lists some assessment measures that are being used to gather information on student achievement of each general education learning outcome, many of which are inexpensive or free.

If an existing assessment measure cannot be located, there are a num-ber of resources available that provide guidance on how to develop your own assessment measure (see Chapter Two of this volume). Although it takes a significant investment of time, developing your own assessment measure can be less expensive than purchasing an existing measure, and it can be one approach for building faculty members' engagement in and ownership of assessment.

Most important, remember that, in the words of Voltaire, "*le mieux est l'ennemi du bien*" (1772, p. A3); "the best is the enemy of the good." The perfect instrument to measure a specific complex general education student learning outcome may never exist. We should continue to work on improving assessment measures for general education student learning outcomes, but we cannot afford to postpone assessment until the perfect measure is developed.

General Education Learning Outcomes Cannot Be Taught. Seymour and Hewitt (1997) found many science, mathematics, and engineering faculty members expected substantial attrition from their programs because "those presumed to lack sufficient natural ability to continue are thought to discover their limitations, and/or their true voca-tion for some other discipline and leave" (p. 7). This view, that academic abilities such as critical thinking or quantitative reasoning cannot be taught and are innate and that the role of higher education is to separate out those who have them and those who do not, may be widely held in many disciplines.

A contrasting view is expressed by Ericsson, Krampe, and Tesch-Römer (1993), who proposed a theoretical framework that "explains expert performance in terms of acquired characteristics resulting from extended deliberate practice and that limits the role of innate (inherited) characteristics to general levels of activity and emotionality" (p. 363). Other researchers have focused on time, not innate ability, as the most essential element related to student achievement (see Finnegan and Hyle, 2009; Gettinger, 1984; Hong and Hong, 2009; and Millot, 1995). Carroll (1963) proposed that a learner "will succeed in learning a given task to the extent that he spends the amount of time that he *needs* to learn the task" (p. 725). Carroll goes on to suggest that perceived differences in students' abilities can be explained by the amount of time required for a particular learning task; students who require a small amount of time to achieve a learning goal have "high aptitude" while those requiring a large amount of time to achieve a learning goal have "low aptitude" (p. 725).

If students, given sufficient time, can become concert violinists and grandmaster chess experts through deliberate practice, then undoubtedly they can also learn to become critical thinkers, quantitative reasoners, and writers through deliberate practice. Given enough time, nearly all of our students are capable of learning anything we would like to teach them.

Results from Assessment of General Education Learning Outcomes Are Never Used for Anything. Too often data from assessment of general education are ignored, abandoned, lost, or simply not used for anything other than proving that assessment was done. There are many reasons assessment data may not be used, among them lack of a shared vision for achievement of the general education learning outcomes, failure to clearly define the general education learning outcomes, failure to gather clear and meaningful assessment data on student achievement of the learning outcomes, distrust in the quality of the assessment measures, lack of faculty members' involvement in the assessment process, and perception that teaching the general education learning outcomes is someone else's responsibility. It does not have to be this way. A number of institutions have been able to overcome these obstacles and as a result transform their general education programs (see Bresciani, 2007). Just because results from assessment of general education may not have been used for anything does not suggest they *cannot* be used.

Assessment of General Education Learning Outcomes Is a Threat to Academic Freedom. Academic freedom is a foundational principle that is essential for achievement of the missions of our institutions. Unfortunately, assessment of general education is often viewed as an external intrusion into the curriculum that limits academic freedom by telling faculty members what and how to teach. Besides, critics contend, we already do assessment through grading.

Yet at its best, assessment of general education supports academic freedom. The *1940 Statement of Principles on Academic Freedom and Tenure* (American Association of University Professors, 1970) is an essential statement that protects the rights of faculty members to teach and perform research freely. These rights come with the responsibility to "seek above all to be effective teachers and scholars" (p. 8). Assessment of general education is an essential element of meeting this responsibility, by establishing a process through which students' achievement of the general education learning outcomes can be studied and improved.

Grading is an essential element of teaching a course and, along with the credit hour, is the currency of higher education. However, grading is at the wrong level for use in determining whether or not students are achieving the general education outcomes and does not always yield useful and meaningful data for improving students' achievement. Even if a common grading scale is used, individual instructors may weight course elements differently. Some faculty members may include attendance or participation as a portion of the grade, while others may include only the results from multiple-choice tests. As a result, interpreting an individual grade or a grade point average as evidence of student achievement of the general education outcomes is problematic. Avoidance of grades as a tool in assessing students' achievement of the general education outcomes is not intended to be a rejection of faculty members' expertise in evaluating student achievement, of the value of course assignments or projects in assessing student achievement of the general education outcomes, or of the central role of courses in students' educational experiences. Rather, it is recognition that course grading serves a different purpose and is not the best way to gather evidence on students' achievement of the general education outcomes.

The Case for Assessment of General Education

Assessment of General Education Has the Potential to Transform Our Institutions. Our institutions are facing many challenges: students are approaching their education in new and unfamiliar ways, colleges are reconceptualizing faculty roles, many of our institutions are facing financial crisis, political pressure for accountability is strong and getting stronger, and students matriculate unprepared and graduate not having learned as much as they should have.

To respond to these and other challenges, institutions must be able to react rapidly and effectively. Yet we know this is not how our institutions are designed. Current structures and processes in our institutions are the result of decades of tradition from which we must struggle mightily for liberation. To make matters worse, many institutions lack a systematic mechanism to use in responding to a changing environment.

Assessment of general education student learning outcomes can be one such mechanism. Assessment of general education becomes a mechanism for transformation by reframing Tyler's guiding questions on curriculum development (1949) into approachable, action-oriented questions, making them a systematic part of institutional self-reflection. These questions become:

1. Are students learning what they should be learning?
2. Which teaching, curricular, and co-curricular approaches are working well, and which approaches need to be modified?
3. What additional educational experiences should be furnished to students, and how should our existing experiences be reorganized?
4. Is our process for assessing general education working effectively?

Many institutions have already experienced transformation through assessment of general education. For example, Coker College developed a new writing effectiveness program, and Alverno College implemented a major redesign of the communications courses (Bresciani, 2007). A college in the State University of New York system received a Title III grant, a community college in the system revised its algebra/precalculus/calculus curriculum, and two additional colleges (one doctoral and one comprehensive) implemented a faculty development program (Bresciani, 2007). Others, such as the University of South Florida, completely reformed the general education program (Bresciani, 2007). North Carolina State University improved teaching through inclusion of service-learning (Banta, Jones, and Black, 2009).

Northeastern Illinois University redeveloped the writing and mathematics curricula (Banta, Jones, and Black, 2009). Oklahoma State University created faculty development initiatives and implemented new writing requirements (Banta, Jones, and Black, 2009). Assessment of general education has already transformed many institutions and has the potential to serve as a mechanism for responding to our changing educational environment.

Assessment of General Education Can Help Meet (Not Always Unreasonable) Expectations for Accountability. We know, from watching students grow in our classes and throughout their degree programs, that earning a degree from our institutions represents a significant achievement that will produce benefits for their future lives and for our communities. This belief is supported by a substantial body of research (Bok, 2006; Cuadras-Morató and Mateors-Planas, 2006; Mortenson, 1999; Pascarella and Terenzini, 2005; U.S. Department of Labor, Bureau of Labor Statistics, 2006). When we are confronted with demands for proof that what we believe is occurring is actually occurring in our institutions as part of an accountability movement, our initial response is often incredulity and anger. Is our professional judgment not sufficient?

At the same time, we recognize many areas of concern. The U.S. Census Bureau estimated in 2007 that 54.4 percent of the U.S. population age twenty-five and older had earned some college credit, but only 27.5 percent had completed a bachelor's degree or higher (U.S. Census Bureau, 2009). The four-year completion rate at public universities is only 28 percent (Higher Education Research Institute, 2005). Learning gains from the freshman to senior year range from 0.24 to 0.90 standard deviations for such areas as mathematical and quantitative skills, subject matter knowledge, and reflective thinking, with a high of 2.0 on epistemological sophistication (Pascarella and Terenzini, 2005). These learning gains are noteworthy, but they are not as large as they could or should be. Former Department of Education Secretary Margaret Spellings summarized these concerns, saying, "It's time to examine how we can get the most out of our national investment [in higher education]" (Spellings, 2005).

Demands for accountability are not always unreasonable. Higher education receives considerable support from taxpayers, totaling nearly $83 billion from state and local taxes in 2007 alone (State Higher Education Executive Officers, 2009). In addition, our institutions are so important to our communities and the individuals we serve that it is not surprising there is a need for evidence on whether or not we are achieving our goals. Although the dialogue about how best to achieve accountability without distorting and corrupting the very thing we are trying to measure is ongoing (see Amrein and Berliner's uncertainty principle, 2002), we cannot, and should not, resist all accountability efforts by labeling them as unreasonable.

Assessment of general education helps us meet expectations for accountability in several ways. First, it produces clear evidence on our students' achievement on learning outcomes that are most central to our institutions. Assessment of general education also facilitates a dialogue about what we expect students to learn in our institutions and identify core knowledge, skills, abilities, and dispositions that are important for all students. At the same time, assessment of general education allows us to exhibit learning and achievements that are unique to each of our institutions, highlighting one of our higher education system's greatest strengths. If used appropriately, assessment of general education can be a meaningful and valuable component of accountability.

Assessment Is Part of Our Responsibility as Faculty Members. There is no better argument for assessment of general education than to say it is the right thing to do. Too often we focus only on the carrot and the stick, forgetting that it is our responsibility as faculty members to ensure that our educational programs are having their desired impact.

Teaching, one of our two primary responsibilities as faculty members (American Association of University Professors, 1970), is made up of three interrelated elements: instruction, curriculum, and assessment. Instructional practices have an impact on the curriculum experienced by our students. Curricular decisions about what educational experiences to offer shape our instructional practices. Assessment informs our instruction by revealing effective and ineffective practices and can also be used as an instructional tool. Assessment reveals whether or not the educational experiences we include in the curriculum are resulting in the desired student achievement. Instruction, curriculum, and assessment are inseparable. We are mistaken if we believe that we can ignore assessment of general education or pass it off to others and still hold on to instruction and curriculum. Assessment of general education may not hold the glamour of research or the gratification of teaching, but it is a critical element of our work as faculty members and can serve an essential element in transforming and improving our institutions.

New Directions for Institutional Research • DOI: 10.1002/ir

References

American Association of University Professors. "1940 Statement of Principles on Academic Freedom and Tenure (with 1970 Interpretive Comments)," 1970. Retrieved March 8, 2010, from http://www.aaup.org/NR/rdonlyres/EBB1B330-33D3-4A51-B534-CEE0C7A90DAB/0/1940StatementofPrinciplesonAcademicFreedomandTenure.pdf.

Amrein, A. L., and Berliner, D. C. "High-Stakes Testing, Uncertainty, and Student Learning." *Education Policy Analysis Archives,* 2002, *10*(18). Retrieved Sept. 11, 2006, from http://epaa.asu.edu/epaa/v10n18/.

Banta, T. W., Jones, E. A., and Black, K. E. *Designing Effective Assessment: Principles and Profiles of Good Practice.* San Francisco: Jossey-Bass, 2009.

Bok, D. *Our Underachieving Colleges: A Candid Look at How Much Students Learn and Why They Should Be Learning More.* Princeton: Princeton University Press, 2006.

Bresciani, M. J. "The Challenges of Assessing General Education: Questions to Consider." In M. J. Bresciani (ed.), *Assessing Student Learning in General Education: Good Practice Case Studies.* Bolton, Mass.: Anker, 2007, 1–15.

Bureau of Labor Statistics. "National Occupational Employment and Wage Estimates: May 2008," 2008. Retrieved March 9, 2010, from http://www.bls.gov/oes/2008/may/oes_nat.htm#b25-0000.

Campbell, D. T., and Fiske, D. W. "Convergent and Discriminant Validation by the Multitrait-Multimethod Matrix." *Psychological Bulletin,* 1959, *56*(2), 81–105.

Carroll, J. B. "A Model of School Learning." *Teachers College Record,* 1963, *64*, 723–733.

Cronbach, L. J. "Construct Validity in Psychological Tests." *Psychological Bulletin,* 1955, *52*(4), 281–302.

Cuadras-Morató, X., and Mateors-Planas, X. "Are Changes in Education Important for the Wage Premium and Unemployment?" *International Economic Review,* 2006, *47*(1), 129–160.

Ericsson, K. A., Krampe, R. T., and Tesch-Römer, C. "The Role of Deliberate Practice in the Acquisition of Expert Performance." *Psychological Review,* 1993, *100*(3), 363–406.

Ewell, P. T. "An Emerging Scholarship: A Brief History of Assessment." In T. W. Banta and Associates (eds.), *Building a Scholarship of Assessment.* San Francisco: Jossey-Bass, 2002, 1–25.

Finnegan, D. E., and Hyle, A. E. "Assistant to 'Full': Rank and the Development of Expertise." *Teachers College Record,* 2009, *111*(2), 443–479.

Gettinger, M. "Achievement as a Function of Time Spent in Learning and Time Needed for Learning." *American Educational Research Journal,* 1984, *21*(3), 617–628.

Hargreaves, A. *Changing Teachers Changing Times: Teachers' Work and Culture in the Postmodern Age.* New York: Teachers College Press, 1994.

Hersh, R. H. "What Does College Teach?" *Atlantic Monthly,* 2005. Retrieved May 26, 2010, from http://assessment.uconn.edu/docs/resources/ARTICLES_and_REPORTS/Richard_Hersh_What_Does_College_Teach.pdf.

Higher Education Research Institute. "How 'Good' is Your Retention Rate? Using the CIRP Survey to Evaluate Undergraduate Persistence," 2005. Retrieved July 24, 2007, from http://gseis.ucla.edu/heri/PDFs/DARCU_RB.PDF.

Hong, G., and Hong, Y. "Reading Instruction Time and Homogeneous Grouping in Kindergarten: An Application of Marginal Mean Weighting Through Stratification." *Educational Evaluation and Policy Analysis,* 2009, *31*(1), 54–81.

Hutchings, P., Marchese, T., and Wright, B. *Using Assessment to Strengthen General Education.* Washington, D.C.: American Association for Higher Education, 1991.

Johnson, D. K., Ratcliff, J. L., and Gaff, J. G. "A Decade of Change in General Education." In *Changing General Education Curriculum.* (Special Issue.) New Directions for Higher Education, no. 125, 2004.

Kramer, P. I. "The Art of Making Assessment Anti-venom: Injecting Assessment in Small Doses to Create a Faculty Culture of Assessment." *Assessment Update,* 2009, *21*(6), 8–10.

Learned, W. S., and Wood, B. D. *The Student and His Knowledge.* New York: Carnegie Foundation for the Advancement of Teaching, 1938.

Maki, P. L. *Assessing for Learning: Building a Sustainable Commitment Across the Institution.* Sterling, Va.: Stylus, 2004.

Millot, B. "Economics of Educational Time and Learning." In M. Carnoy (ed.), *International Encyclopedia of Economics Education.* Oxford, UK: Pergamon-Elsevier, 1995.

Mortenson, T. G. "Why College? Private Correlates of Educational Attainment." *Postsecondary Education Opportunity,* 1999, *81,* 1–24.

Mulcahy, D. G. *The Educated Person: Toward a New Paradigm for Liberal Education.* Lanham, Md.: Rowman and Littlefield, 2008.

National Leadership Council for Liberal Education and America's Promise. *College Learning for the New Global Century.* Washington, DC: Association of American Colleges and Universities, 2007.

Newman, J. H. C. *The Idea of a University* (ed. C. F. Harrold). New York: Longmans, Green, 1947.

Pascarella, E. T., and Terenzini, P. T. *How College Affects Students: A Third Decade of Research* (vol. 2). San Francisco: Jossey-Bass, 2005.

Pinar, W. F., Reynolds, W. M., Slattery, P., and Taubman, P. M. *Understanding Curriculum: An Introduction to the Study of Historical and Contemporary Curriculum Discourses.* New York: Peter Lang, 1996.

Schwyzer, H. (2007). "The Educrats' Attack on Teaching." InsideHigherEd.com. Retrieved Oct. 8, 2007, from http://www.insidehighered.com/views/2007/10/08/schwyzer.

Seymour, E., and Hewitt, N. M. *Talking About Leaving: Why Undergraduates Leave the Sciences.* Boulder, Colo.: Westview, 1997.

Spellings, M. "Prepared Remarks for Secretary Spellings at the Meeting of the Commission on the Future of Higher Education," Sept. 19, 2005. Charlotte, North Carolina. Retrieved April 1, 2007, from http://www2.ed.gov/news/speeches/2005/09/09192005.html.

State Higher Education Executive Officers. "State Higher Education Finance: FY 2009," 2009. Retrieved March 9, 2010, from http://www.sheeo.org/finance/shef/SHEF_FY_2009.pdf.

Study Group on the Conditions of Excellence in American Higher Education. *Involvement in Learning: Realizing the Potential of American Higher Education.* Washington, D.C.: National Institute of Education, 1984.

Tyler, R. W. *Basic Principles of Curriculum and Instruction.* Chicago: University of Chicago Press, 1949.

U.S. Census Bureau. "Educational Attainment in the United States: 2007," 2009. Retrieved March 1,, 2011, from http://www.census.gov/prod/2009pubs/p20-560.pdf.

U.S. Department of Labor, Bureau of Labor Statistics. "Employment Status of the Civilian Noninstitutional Population 25 Years and over by Educational Attainment, Sex, Race, and Hispanic or Latino Ethnicity, 2006. Retrieved July 24, 2007, from http://www.stats.bls.gov/cps/cpsaat7.pdf.

Voltaire (Arouet, F.-M.). *La Bégueule: Conte moral,* 1772. Retrieved July 12, 2010, from http://www.archive.org/details/labgueulecontem00voltgoog.

JEREMY D. PENN *is the director of assessment and testing and an adjunct faculty member in the School of Educational Studies at Oklahoma State University.*

2

This chapter outlines a systematic process for developing assessment measures for complex outcomes that is based on a rigorous research approach used by psychologists.

Outcome Assessment from the Perspective of Psychological Science: The TAIM Approach

Pamela Steinke, Peggy Fitch

If outcomes assessment is ever to become an integral part of how institutions of higher education function, the process must be rooted in scholarship and fit the culture and core mission of the academy. The problems that result from an approach that is not rooted in scholarship become particularly salient when assessing complex outcomes central to the institution, including general education outcomes; outcomes of quality enhancement initiatives, such as the Academic Quality Improvement Program (AQIP) or Quality Enhancement Plan (QEP); and institutional outcomes that follow directly from the mission, vision, and core values of the institution.

The complexity of these types of outcomes often leaves faculty members and administrators uncertain about how to assess them. Fueled by fears of not passing reaccreditation, they are tempted to opt for the certainty of *measurable* outcomes rather than exploring measures of *meaningful* outcomes. This misguided search for measurable rather than meaningful outcomes can lead to precise measurement of outcomes that are not central to the institution and do little or nothing to improve student learning or the overall quality of the institution. To develop meaningful outcomes, it is important for an institution or program to clearly identify what it is about, why it exists, and who it wants to be *before* entering into conversations about measurement. Too often, staff members in offices of assessment or institutional research discourage this introspective

NEW DIRECTIONS FOR INSTITUTIONAL RESEARCH, no. 149, Spring 2011 © Wiley Periodicals, Inc.
Published online in Wiley Online Library (wileyonlinelibrary.com) • DOI: 10.1002/ir.377

approach, pushing instead for selection of easily measurable outcomes because of concerns that measuring complex outcomes will lead to sticky, complicated measurement issues or will take too long. The seduction of clean measurement, where the measures have unequivocal validity and reliability and the results are unambiguous, is itself an illusion when it comes to assessment. Data will never be perfect and can never speak for themselves. The less meaningful the outcomes, however, the less likely it is that the assessment data will actually be used, no matter how clean they are.

In this chapter, we outline an approach to assessing complex constructs supported by psychological science and research. This approach is informed by our background as psychologists but is general enough to incorporate other disciplinary approaches as well. We identify this approach as TAIM (Theory, Activities, Indicators, Multiple Measures) to highlight the main assumptions of the approach. We believe that *theory* and research should inform assessment throughout the process, that clarity on intentional instructional *activities* is essential, that definitions of outcomes are not complete without specifying *indicators*, and that complex outcomes need *multiple measures*. Our background as psychologists informs not only each of these assumptions but also the broader framework of the TAIM approach.

The Framework of the TAIM Approach

Outcomes assessment is often portrayed as a cycle that includes (1) identifying outcomes, (2) gathering evidence, (3) interpreting evidence, and (4) implementing change (Maki, 2004). In a similar fashion, the cycle of scientific inquiry is typically portrayed as a process that includes (1) a theory, (2) generating hypotheses to test the theory, (3) and making observations by collecting data that are analyzed for the purpose of (4) refining the theory (Kantowitz, Roediger, and Elmes, 2009). There are a number of parallels between the assessment cycle and the cycle of scientific inquiry (see Fig. 2.1). We think of assessment as a form of action research for the purpose of solving the immediate problem of how to enhance outcomes through enlisting the help of those closest to the problem. As action research, outcomes assessment can be viewed as a type of research that does not always have tight controls. For example, it usually does not allow random assignment or even measurement of many confounding factors, but it is scholarly research nonetheless. We advocate for controls to ensure that data are as clean as possible, but we also do not accept the argument that having no data is better than having imperfect data. Multiple measures along with the use of critical thinking when interpreting the data should offset imperfect data.

Furthermore, we use findings in psychology to define the institutional environment within which the TAIM approach best functions. At the

Figure 2.1. Parallels Between the Cycle of Assessment and the Cycle of Scientific Inquiry

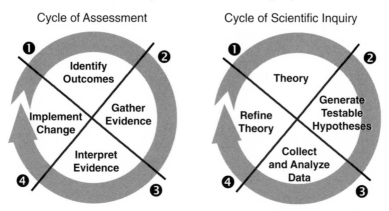

institutional level, moving toward the TAIM approach requires resources, structure, and leadership support beyond the efforts of individual faculty or practitioners. If assessment is to be owned by faculty and practitioners, it must be supported as a scholarly enterprise. This recognition includes support for professional development in assessment as part of teaching; recognition of the scholarship of assessment as part of the scholarship of teaching and learning; and inclusion in load, tenure, and promotion decisions and recognition events (Hutchings, 2010). Many current personality researchers in the area of positive psychology emphasize the nature of humans as goal-directed and the importance of goals for emotional survival and well-being (Snyder and Lopez, 2002). Assessment processes must engage faculty and staff in their professional capacity as the goal-driven beings they are, if they are expected to remain motivated throughout the process.

The culture of the institution also requires consistent messaging about the intrinsic importance of assessment for continuous enhancement of how the institution functions in order to achieve its mission beyond any extrinsic accreditation pressures. Much educational research has demonstrated a relationship between goal orientation and goal attainment (see Pintrich, 2000). When goal performance is motivated by the desire to gain extrinsic rewards such as passing accreditation or pleasing one's supervisor, persistence and mastery-level performance are much harder to attain than when goal performance is motivated by intrinsic factors such as the desire to improve student learning or to increase one's competence in a given area. Motivation by extrinsic factors alone will often lead to putting off efforts until the last minute, doing what has to get done "to get by," and dropping off efforts when the extrinsic motivators are no longer present. Unfortunately, there is no better example of this than assessment efforts in relationship to accreditation cycles. This does not mean that extrinsic motivators such as accreditation pressures are harmful; rather, educational research suggests that as long as intrinsic motivation is present, extrinsic motivators will not hurt and will often help. Although assessment motivated purely by extrinsic factors describes the current state of many faculty members (Hutchings, 2010), those who have embraced outcomes-based education are reaching a much higher level of competency in assessment (Driscoll and Wood, 2007; Mentkowski and Associates, 2000). When intrinsic motivation is present, the tension between the ideal outcome state and the current state based on feedback from assessment data will provide the impetus for taking specific actions for improvement.

At the departmental or program level, intrinsic motivation will fuel the drive to keep focused on outcomes. It is important, therefore, that outcomes not be stated too specifically, requiring a laundry list of outcomes to encompass the breadth of a given program. Focusing on a smaller, more meaningful, broader set helps programs keep outcomes in focus. Cognitive psychological research on short-term memory supports a smaller, meaningful set of outcomes as well. Beginning with the classic paper by George Miller (1956), discussion of short-term memory often identifies the limit as seven, plus or minus two, meaningful chunks of information. Outcomes should be so central to the program or institution that they can be recalled without difficulty. Too many faculty and administrators keep their outcomes at arm's length, as if they are secondary to the functioning of the program. Some indications of this are lack of clear relationships between mission and outcomes, faculty and staff members not knowing what the outcomes are, outcomes not being clearly posted on the website or other external communications, outcomes not being shared with current students, and outcomes not forming the basis of discussion in departmental, program, or institutional retreats.

In addition to our use of theory and research to inform the framework of the TAIM approach, the approach itself asks faculty and practitioners responsible for assessment to engage in a scholarly process when they do assessment. This process fits with the culture of higher education and encourages professional scholarship.

T = Theory and Research. The TAIM approach begins with using theory and research as tools to inform outcome development. This means that a program's outcomes should be informed by disciplinary, topical, or pedagogical theory and research. Institutions of higher education produce valuable research and theory on topics such as global understanding and problem solving; yet these same institutions sometimes do not rely on this theory and research when they approach their own outcomes assessment. This disconnect highlights the problem with assessment when it is not integrated into the culture of the academy.

The TAIM approach does not require that representatives from each program become experts in every outcome area. Support can be elicited from faculty and staff on campus who already have this expertise; easily accessible, digestible summaries of scholarly work can form the basis of discussion (see the chapters in Part Two of this volume for some examples). We do not suggest that all involved must develop a scholarly interest in the outcome areas; rather, we ask of faculty and staff what we ask of our students, that is, to support their assertions with evidence.

Nor does this mean that theory and research have to inform all discussions of outcomes, or that programs should not start with simple brainstorming. One of the best ways to begin any conversation about outcomes is to bring all members of a department or program together and ask such questions as "Imagine an ideal graduate from your program. What kinds of skills, knowledge, or other attributes characterize that graduate?" or "What value does this program offer a student?" (Carter, 2002, p. 15). The TAIM approach suggests that during the process of outcome development, as these main attributes are identified, further understanding of what they mean and how to measure them should be informed by theory, research, and other professional scholarship in the field, always situated within the context of the institution. If outcome development is informed by theory and research, there will necessarily be additional resources for outcome measurement as strategies and indicators are identified.

A = Activities/Strategies. In addition to being grounded in scholarly work, assessment must also be aligned with intentional practices that target student achievement of the outcomes. The intentionality of teaching to outcomes is a fundamental assumption of outcomes assessment; thus explicit alignment between activities or strategies and outcomes is crucial.

Curriculum mapping is one popular way of ensuring that the overall curriculum is aligned with outcomes (see Suskie, 2009), but too often this is done by simply asking faculty members to say whether or at what level an outcome is addressed in each course without specifying how it is addressed. Curriculum mapping can be useful for ensuring that there is a developmental progression in how the outcomes are addressed, such that they are first introduced, then practiced, and then demonstrated. A curriculum map, however, does not reveal how intentionally the outcomes are taught. Strategies used within courses, experiential, and co-curricular programs more clearly identify intentional practices. A curriculum or program map can still be a good place to start, but ultimately the map should go beyond simply mapping the curriculum or program, to looking at how specific strategies are used and considering how academic and co-curricular activities may be integrated.

This is where specific/strategic, measurable, attainable, results-oriented, and time-bound (SMART) goals can be appropriate—in specifying strategies as action steps. SMART goals worked for action steps in business and were subsequently adopted by K–12 education (see O'Neill, 2000). More recently they have been used to help professionals in higher education write measurable outcomes. Although SMART goals can help specify activities or action steps for achieving outcomes, assessment of meaningful complex outcomes requires extension beyond the SMART model. SMART goals can be useful for identifying action steps in the assessment process, but this is not the same as using them to write outcomes. The type of outcomes that much of higher education is intended to address are most often general rather than specific (Association of American Colleges and Universities, AACU, 2008) and transferable across time and context rather than time-bound (Barnett and Ceci, 2002). To simplify outcomes too much is to deny responsibility for teaching students deep learning, higher-order thinking skills, and application of knowledge to future contexts, which is precisely the function of higher education (Bok, 2006).

Activities or action steps differ from outcomes in other important ways. Outcomes should be relatively stable; that is, programs do not generally change what they are about from year to year. However, action steps need to be fluid and changing; they are the strategies that are changed in order to enhance student outcomes as faculty members and practitioners close the assessment loop between gathering data and making enhancements. In psychological science, activities are analogous to treatments or potential causal factors that are measured or manipulated (independent variables) to see whether they have an effect on the variables of interest (dependent variables). Just as researchers engage in continuous dialogue about the effects of the independent variables on the dependent variables, being intentional about potentially causal strategies designed to improve student outcomes requires engaging in continuous dialogue with colleagues. Aligning activities with outcomes can also help begin the process of identifying indicators and measures.

I = Indicators/Criteria. Specifying indicators of student achievement of identified outcomes is a crucial, yet underused, step in outcomes assessment. Programs often assume that the process of crafting complicated statements on expected student learning outcomes is equivalent to defining outcomes, and that the process automatically achieves shared understanding of their meanings. However, without clear consensus on a set of criteria or indicators that specify demonstration of the outcomes, it will be difficult to identify valid measures and sustain interest in the results.

Driscoll and Wood (2007) describe a process for working with faculty to identify indicators that involves faculty members stating the often-unarticulated criteria that they use in judging student work. Specification of clear indicators or criteria parallels formation of operational definitions in psychological science. For example, psychologists recognize that meaningful, messy constructs such as love can be defined in numerous ways—by the score on a scale, by a physiological response, by a specific behavior—but they never assume that the definition itself is the construct. The assessment literature has sometimes confused definitions and outcomes by encouraging development of outcomes as operational definitions, which again encourages outcomes that are narrow, context-specific, and time-bound and ultimately disconnected from the mission of the program or institution.

Specifying indicators of outcomes will help identify assessment measures. For example, the Valid Assessment of Learning in Undergraduate Education (VALUE) rubrics were created for the Liberal Education and America's Promise (LEAP) outcomes (AACU, 2009). In the problem-solving rubric, the criteria—defining the problem, identifying strategies, proposing solutions or hypotheses, evaluating potential solutions, implementing solutions and evaluating outcomes—are the indicators, whereas the levels—benchmark, milestones, and capstone—are the measures of those indicators. Many other indicators could also be generated for problem solving. However, it is not necessary to measure every indicator, just as in psychological research it is not necessary to measure every operational definition.

Indicators could refer to standards or benchmarks explicitly, but this is not necessary. In the example above, a program may specify that 80 percent of students will be at the capstone level of evaluating potential solutions. However, if this benchmark of 80 percent is set arbitrarily, then it will serve to simply focus discussion on what the results say about this arbitrary benchmark instead of what they say about the meaningful outcome. Another problem with benchmarks is that they often encourage interpretation of the data in terms of whether the benchmark was or was not met, rather than in terms of how the data are useful for enhancement. This is where assessment for learning could be viewed as deviating from psychological science. In quantitative research, psychologists set up research questions so they can accept or reject the null hypothesis that there was no effect of an independent variable on a dependent variable. This is typically done through use of inferential statistics and effect sizes. As assessment becomes more sophisticated, faculty and practitioners may choose to do some of these inferential analyses and specify hypotheses, but this would not require using benchmarks. This is a promising way to improve the quality of assessment and help faculty and practitioners integrate their scholarship with their assessment work (Hutchings, 2010).

With or without benchmarks or inferential analyses, data need to be interpreted within some context (Suskie, 2009). Approaching quantitative or qualitative assessment as action research allows examination of the data through multiple perspectives or lenses, such as trends over time, evidence of value added, comparison with similar institutions, comparison with other departments within the institution, and strengths and weaknesses of student skills. Each of these perspectives entails a slightly different interpretation. Just as multiple methods are recommended, so are multiple perspectives or lenses on the same data (Suskie, 2009).

Finally, activities or strategies should be directed at enhancing not the indicator itself but rather the broader outcome. For example, students' questions in class may be an indicator of self-regulated learning. It would not, however, be a valid strategy to increase self-regulated learning by simply getting students to ask more questions with whatever means are available, such as extra credit. Sometimes this happens with survey data. Programs specify an indicator that is measured by a survey question and includes a benchmark, such as 90 percent of respondents agreeing or strongly agreeing with the survey item. Survey results may serve as a valid indicator, but if the focus is on raising survey scores rather than improving outcomes, then questions on the survey might be phrased such that almost anyone would have to agree ("I was exposed to the topic" rather than "I feel confident that I understand the topic well enough to be able to apply it in my daily life"). The other problem with teaching to the indicator instead of the outcome is that a given indicator may measure multiple constructs, such as both motivation and skill, which is one reason multiple measures are always recommended.

M = Multiple Measures. When outcomes remain broad and represent complex constructs, they require multiple measures. One of the most common ways to stray from meaningful outcomes assessment is to try to find "the one" measure for each construct. There is never one true measure of a complex construct. Outcomes can be thought of as latent constructs, which are never visible directly, whereas indicators are manifest and therefore can be directly linked to measures. Latent variable models assume that empirical models of human behavior require consideration of the relationships between multiple variables, some of which are unobserved (Loehlin, 1987). The goal of quantitative analyses in assessment or institutional research is to uncover causal relationships or patterns between multiple variables (Toutkoushian, 2007), so latent variable models are often a better fit than experimental designs. The importance of multiple measures does not suggest that outcomes assessment needs to become unmanageable such that more data are being collected than can be reasonably reviewed. If there are only a few meaningful outcomes, this will allow each outcome to have multiple data sources without the process becoming unmanageable.

Once meaningful measures are found that provide good feedback for enhancement, major changes to these assessments will not need to be made every year. Further, many sources of data can permit several measures. For example, team member, self, and instructor scores could be generated from a single rubric, and a student's self-reflection piece could be read as an indirect measure and scored by an expert for direct evidence of cognitive skills (Steinke and Fitch, 2007). Moreover, the work of assessment does not need to be done by a single department. Getting faculty, practitioners, and students involved across the institution can turn an interesting assessment approach into a research project (Hutchings, 2010).

Each step in the TAIM approach, including measures, can be informed by theory and research. For example, scales and tests may have been developed on the basis of theoretical or empirical constructs. Many scales developed by scholars and published in journals can be used free with permission of the author. This was the approach taken with several measures from the Wabash National Study (Wabash College Center of Inquiry, 2010). Scholarly work can also be used to create survey questions, criteria for a rubric, items on a behavioral checklist, focus group questions, peer evaluations, or other assessment tools.

Both quantitative and qualitative data are often needed if one is to feel confident enough in the results to recommend specific enhancements. In some cases, quantitative data will yield information on what is happening, but without giving context to the quantitative data in the form of qualitative data it will be unclear why it is happening (Howard and Borland, 2007). It is also important to consider what type of data will make the most sense to those reviewing it. Furnishing multiple charts of quantitative data to colleagues who think qualitatively may not be as productive as offering mostly qualitative data with a few quantitative findings.

Thinking widely about all those besides the instructor who can give feedback on the indicators will also help to identify measures. Student self-assessment not only has the potential to constitute an important source of data for assessment, but it also can be integral to students' learning and development (Mentkowski and Associates, 2000). Responses of knowledgeable others on campus, including other faculty and staff members and students' peers, can be another excellent data source. Community members, including alumni, employers, field supervisors, and other professionals in the discipline, can also supply very useful information.

Finally, it is important to use relevant institutional data that are already being collected at the institution for other purposes. The institutional research office can make data for assessment available from institutional databases, from special institutional surveys such as the National Survey of Student Engagement (NSSE), and from national databases, such as data from the National Student Clearinghouse or the Integrated Postsecondary Educational Data System or IPEDS (Toutkoushian, 2007).

Conclusion

In this chapter we have presented an approach to assessment that is grounded in psychological theory and research and that is consistent with the culture of higher education. It is an approach that seeks to engage faculty and practitioners in the practice of assessment because it takes this practice seriously as a scholarly enterprise. Assessment can no longer afford to be done outside of the theory and research that are the products of institutions of higher education; nor can it afford to be done outside the performance criteria for faculty and professional staff. Nearly two-thirds of institutions surveyed struggle with faculty engagement in assessment (Kuh and Ikenberry, 2009). As Hutchings (2010) writes, "Much of what has been done in the name of assessment has failed to engage large numbers of faculty in significant ways" (p. 6). If one of the outcomes for assessment is that faculty will have ownership of the process, then what we are currently doing is not working and we need to make improvements soon.

The urgency of change in assessment practice is rooted in the inauthentic way in which current assessment practice claims to represent reality. The Association of American Colleges and Universities has championed a wake-up call for more meaningful outcomes and measures, and it is clear that the public, including employers, agree (AACU, 2008). The stakes of ignoring the lack of authenticity in many current assessment practices are high. The United States is falling behind in terms of delineating and assessing outcomes that represent the most important skills and knowledge students have for success, calling into question the assumption that the system of higher education in this country is of the highest quality in the world (see Bok, 2006; Hersh and Merrow, 2005).

Recognizing that assessment must be grounded in scholarship will help to further the inherent relationship between assessment and professional development. Faculty and staff are often alienated from the process of assessment because assessment is not well integrated with their professional development. As Driscoll and Wood (2007) note, "It is important to recognize that assessment and the consequent improvement in teaching and learning must remain in the hands of faculty instructors rather than administrators or outside testing agencies" (p. 17). If faculty and staff are going to be empowered to make improvements, assessment and professional development must be intimately connected, adequately resourced, and locally owned; yet few institutions are currently structured to make full use of this relationship.

Ending at M in TAIM does not close the loop between results and enhancements, but it does get to this gap meaningfully. Once data from multiple measures have been collected, they must be shared and discussed among colleagues until they are comfortable with recommending and implementing enhancements based on the data. Ongoing quality assessment depends on a clear plan for how the assessment data will be used. Without meaningful outcomes and engagement in the process, however, ownership and responsibility for the enhancements will not be achieved. It is our hope that by following the TAIM approach those who need to sit down with the data will be motivated to do so because they own the process as academicians and scholars.

References

Association of American Colleges and Universities (AACU). "College Learning for the New Global Century." National Leadership Council for Liberal Education and America's Promise. Washington, D.C.: AACU, 2008.

Association of American Colleges and Universities (AACU). "The VALUE Project Overview." *Peer Review: Emerging Trends and Key Debates in Undergraduate Education*, 2009, *11*(1), 4–7.

Barnett, S., and Ceci, S. J. "When and Where Do We Apply What We Learn? A Taxonomy for Far Transfer." *Psychological Bulletin*, 2002, *128*(4), 612–637.

Bok, D. *Our Underachieving Colleges: A Candid Look at How Much Students Learn and Why They Should Be Learning More*. Princeton, N.J.: Princeton University Press, 2006.

Carter, M. "A Process for Establishing Outcomes-Based Assessment Plans for Writing and Speaking in the Disciplines." *Language and Learning Across the Disciplines*, 2002, *6*(1), 4–29.

Driscoll, A., and Wood, S. *Outcomes-Based Assessment for Learner-Centered Education: A Faculty Introduction*. Sterling, Va.: Stylus, 2007.

Hersh, R. H., and Merrow, J. *Declining by Degrees*. New York: Palgrave Macmillan, 2005.

Howard, R. D., and Borland, K. W. "The Role of Mixed Method Approaches in Institutional Research." In R. D. Howard (ed.), *Using Mixed Methods in Institutional Research*. Tallahassee, Fla.: Association for Institutional Research, 2007.

Hutchings, P. "Opening Doors to Faculty Involvement in Assessment," 2010. National Institute for Learning Outcomes Assessment, occasional paper no. 4. Retrieved May 20, 2010, from http://www.learningoutcomeassessment.org/documents/PatHutchings.pdf.

Kantowitz, B. H., Roediger, H. L., and Elmes, D. G. *Experimental Psychology: Understanding Psychological Research* (9th ed.). Belmont, Calif.: Wadsworth, 2009.

Kuh, G., and Ikenberry, S. "More Than You Think, Less Than We Need: Learning Outcomes Assessment in American Higher Education," 2009. National Institute for Learning Outcomes Assessment. Retrieved May 20, 2010, from http://www.learningoutcomeassessment.org/NILOAsurveyresults09.htm.

Loehlin, J. C. *Latent Variable Models: An Introduction to Factor, Path, and Structural Analysis*. Mahwah, N.J.: Erlbaum, 1987.

Maki, P. L. *Assessing for Learning: Building a Sustainable Commitment Across the Institution*. Sterling, Va.: Stylus, 2004.

Mentkowski, M., and Associates. *Learning That Lasts: Integrating Learning, Development, and Performance in College and Beyond*. San Francisco: Jossey-Bass, 2000.

Miller, G. "The Magical Number Seven, Plus or Minus Two: Some Limits on Our Capacity for Processing Information." *Psychological Review*, 1956, *63*, 81–97.

O'Neill, J. "SMART Goals, SMART Schools." *Educational Leadership*, 2000, *57*(5), 46–50.

Pintrich, P. R. "Multiple Goals, Multiple Pathways: The Role of Goal Orientation in Learning and Achievement." *Journal of Educational Psychology*, 2000, *92*(3), 544–555.

Snyder, C. R., and Lopez. S. J. (eds.). *Handbook of Positive Psychology*. New York: Oxford University Press, 2002.

Steinke, P., and Fitch, P. "Assessing Service-Learning." *Research and Practice in Assessment*, 2007, *1*(2), 1–8. Retrieved May 20, 2010 from http://www.virginiaassessment.org/rpa/2/Steinke%20Fitch.pdf.

Suskie, L. *Assessing Student Learning: A Common Sense Guide* (2nd ed.). San Francisco: Jossey-Bass, 2009.

Toutkoushian, R. K. "The Use of Quantitative Analysis for Institutional Research." In R. D. Howard (ed.), *Using Mixed Methods in Institutional Research*. Tallahassee, Fla.: Association for Institutional Research, 2007.

Wabash College Center of Inquiry. "Wabash National Study," 2010. Retrieved May 20, 2010, from http://www.liberalarts.wabash.edu/study-instruments/.

PAMELA STEINKE *is the director of research, planning, and assessment at Meredith College in Raleigh, North Carolina; her scholarly interests include cognitive outcomes of service-learning and outcomes assessment.*

PEGGY FITCH *is a professor of psychology at Central College in Pella, Iowa; her research interests include service-learning, intellectual development, assessment, and development of intercultural competence.*

NEW DIRECTIONS FOR INSTITUTIONAL RESEARCH • DOI: 10.1002/ir

PART TWO

Application

3

This chapter presents suggestions for assessing critical thinking based on eighteen years of assessing the critical thinking component of Baker University's freshman critical thinking and writing sequence. The data indicate that an institution can expect assessment results to depend on which test one chooses and whose scores are reported.

Which Test? Whose Scores? Comparing Standardized Critical Thinking Tests

Donald L. Hatcher

Critical thinking (CT) is often listed in college catalogues as one of an institution's educational goals. According to Derek Bok (2006), "Nationwide polls have found that more than 90% of faculty members in the U.S. consider it [CT] the most important purpose of undergraduate education" (pp. 67–68). Although enhancing students' CT skills and dispositions is surely a worthy outcome, such a goal creates a number of challenges. First, faculties must decide on a defensible conception of CT. As those familiar with the literature know, this is no easy task. There are many conceptions, and each implies a slightly different set of skills or emphases (Hatcher, 2000; Lipman, 2006).

Once faculty members have agreed on the relevant skills, they must next confront the added challenge of choosing an appropriate assessment tool. If faculty members do not want to go down the laborious paths of collecting and evaluating student portfolios (Possin, 2008), or creating and attempting to validate their own assessment instrument, then they must choose from the numerous standardized critical-thinking tests that are on the market, administer the test, record pretest and posttest scores, and if possible perform an error analysis to determine which areas of student performance were weakest. Finally, after this process, faculty members are challenged to determine the strengths and weaknesses of their attempts to teach CT skills and adjust their pedagogy accordingly.

The author would like to thank Molly Ireland, his accomplished student assistant, for grading hundreds of CCTST tests, entering the names and data on spreadsheets, and doing the statistics found throughout this chapter.

NEW DIRECTIONS FOR INSTITUTIONAL RESEARCH, no. 149, Spring 2011 © Wiley Periodicals, Inc.
Published online in Wiley Online Library (wileyonlinelibrary.com) • DOI: 10.1002/ir.378

29

In this chapter, after describing one approach for teaching CT that was in place at Baker University from 1990 to 2008, I describe our experience assessing CT using three standardized exams and show why the choice of a standardized CT test can be problematic and the results misleading. These results can be misleading because the effect size gains (defined as the mean gain expressed as a percentage of a standard deviation) on critical thinking tests can vary significantly, even under ideal conditions where the course, text, and teachers remain relatively the same throughout a lengthy assessment period. In addition, the data indicate a wide disparity of student gains relative to their instructors. As a consequence, the assessment results may vary greatly depending on which test is chosen or whose scores are reported. At a time when some suggest that an institution's test results be made public (U.S. Department of Education, 2006), this comparison of three common tests of CT should be helpful. Although there has been research employing each of the three standardized CT tests used at Baker (Ennis, Millman, and Tomko, 2004; Hatcher 1999a, 1999b, 2006; Hitchcock, 2004; Solon, 2003; van Gelder, Cumming, and Bissett, 2004), no study has focused on the question of whether these three widely used tests (the Ennis-Weir Critical Thinking Essay Test, the California Critical Thinking Skills Test, and the Cornell Critical Thinking Test, Level Z) are similar in reporting student performance. Without such knowledge, one might think that one's favored approach to teaching CT was yielding terrific results, when in fact if one used another assessment instrument the results would be quite different. Therefore, clear guidance on choosing a test that best fits how one understands CT and which skills are to be tested is essential.

One Approach for Teaching CT: Baker University's Liberal Arts Program

From 1990 to 2008, Baker University's General Education Program included three specially designed core courses: a two-semester freshman sequence and a senior capstone course. The courses in the freshman sequence, "Critical Thinking and Effective Writing" and "Ideas and Exposition," integrated instruction in logic and critical thinking with researching and writing position papers. The senior capstone course, "Science, Technology, and Human Values," required seniors to choose a public policy issue created by current developments in science or technology and then research, prepare, present, and defend a substantial position paper arguing for a specific public policy. Special emphasis was placed on responding to possible objections to the proposed position. Areas included scientific research, energy policy, medical technologies, and defense policy, to name a few of many. Although the remainder of the General Education Program consisted of distribution requirements, in an attempt to encourage CT across the curriculum the majority of Baker's faculty members attended summer workshops that covered the CT and writing material taught to all freshmen (Hatcher and Spencer, 2006).

The senior capstone course began in 1979. Soon, teachers complained that many seniors were seriously challenged by such an assignment. Students were found deficient in constructing and evaluating arguments that would constitute the core of their papers. In 1988, with the help of two FIPSE grants from the U.S. Department of Education ($68,500 and $106,110), faculty members from the humanities began planning the two-semester freshman critical-thinking and writing sequence. From 1991 to 2005, various parts of the program were sustained and enhanced by four generous grants (totaling $866,000) from the Hall Family Foundation.

Defining CT. The first challenge for those planning the new courses was agreeing on a definition of CT. This definition would, to a large extent, guide both the structure and the content of the courses. Various standard definitions were considered, but none were found satisfactory (Hatcher, 2000). The definition needed to be clear and concise so that all faculty members would know what we were talking about when we proposed adopting the new course sequence. The definition should make it clear why CT is an essential educational goal and how our courses were designed to achieve that goal. It should also indicate the criteria used to evaluate claims; otherwise, people would disagree on what counts for a reasonable position. Additionally, the definition should allow people to distinguish CT from other cognitive skills such as creative thinking, problem solving, and logic.

Given these constraints and the goal of integrating instruction in CT and writing, we agreed on this definition: critical thinking is "thinking that tries to arrive at a judgment only after honestly evaluating alternatives with respect to available evidence and arguments" (Hatcher and Spencer, 2006, p. 1). This definition gave the needed foundation to a course integrating instruction in critical thinking and writing. That is, if a student is assigned a position paper, it requires that the writing process include honest evaluation of alternative positions before choosing the one to be defended—not a novel idea in both inquiry and argumentation (Govier, 1999; Johnson, 1996, 2000, 2009; Mill, 1978).

Teaching and Assessing CT. The two courses in the freshman sequence differed from traditional critical-thinking courses insofar as they emphasized the use of formal logic and critical-thinking skills to enhance student writing (Hatcher, 1999a). Throughout the two semesters of the freshman sequence, the time spent on writing far exceeded the time spent on logic. These courses also differed from traditional written composition courses in emphasizing only the argumentative essay, with special emphasis on treating possible objections and replies.

The first course in the freshman sequence began by explaining the nature and importance of critical thinking. Students read Plato's "Allegory of the Cave," in hopes they would see how many of their beliefs and values were not the product of a thoughtful evaluation of alternatives but rather the result of whatever ideas and values were promoted in their specific "caves" when they were young.

The importance of critical thinking was followed by instruction in basic critical-thinking skills, among them summarizing and evaluating arguments, and using knowledge of valid deductive argument patterns to construct strong arguments for their papers. Once arguments were properly summarized, they were evaluated by a technique called *deductive reconstruction* (Cederblom and Paulsen, 2006; Nosich, 1982). Deductive reconstruction asks students to restructure each argument into a valid deductive form (usually *modus ponens* or *modus tollens*). Then, for evaluation purposes, the main question is whether the premises are reasonable and relevant to the conclusion, which usually involves understanding what makes for good inductive inferences, as well as a degree of information literacy. Instruction in basic logic lasted only until midsemester—an unusually brief period for a CT course.

The last half of the first semester freshman course focused on applying the logical tools of deductive reconstruction to writing papers. Students were asked to construct the strongest arguments they could on both sides of an issue and then evaluate those arguments. They then chose the most defensible position and constructed a thesis and outline for their papers. Students met with their instructor to discuss the outlines, focusing on both the strength of the arguments given in support of their thesis and whether the arguments on the other side had been given a fair treatment. If the outline was acceptable, they then began work on a draft. On completion of the draft, another conference was scheduled between the student and instructor. All papers followed the same five-part pattern (even though the order may vary), with an introduction, clarification and thesis, supporting reasons and arguments, possible objections and replies, and then a summation and conclusion. In the second semester of the freshman sequence, students applied these critical-thinking skills and writing strategies to five sets of readings, writing five additional papers, all including the same components described above.

The papers were assessed using a rubric that had been agreed on by all faculty members teaching the courses in the sequence that assessed students' CT and writing skills. In addition to use of the rubric, we were instructed by our consultant, Stephen Norris, to use standardized tests with pretest and posttesting to assess critical-thinking skills.

Faculty development and collaboration was essential because there were twelve to fourteen sections of the freshman sequence each semester, taught by faculty members from a variety of departments. New teachers were asked to attend a week-long summer workshop to work through the material in the CT and writing text. For the first semester, there were weekly staff meetings to go over the material to be covered the following week, and discussion on which teaching practices were working well or not so well.

This approach to teaching CT was what those who planned the courses considered a reasonable solution to the initial problem of preparing seniors for their capstone projects. The papers in the freshman year were similar to miniature versions of the senior project. It was a novel approach at the time (hence the two FIPSE grants); most instruction in CT involved use of logic texts, both formal and informal, and did not emphasize writing.

Baker University's Experience Assessing CT

Careful assessment was required because the freshman program was funded by two FIPSE grants. Following the advice of Stephen Norris, coauthor with Bob Ennis of *Evaluating Critical Thinking* (1989), we began assessing the critical-thinking element of the courses using the Ennis-Weir Critical Thinking Essay Test (E-W; Ennis and Weir, 1985). The university deemed this test the best option because the course sequence integrated instruction in writing with critical thinking. The E-W asks students to respond in writing to an eight-paragraph letter to the editor, telling whether the reasoning in each paragraph is good or bad, to support their judgment with reasons, and to generate a final paragraph evaluating the overall argument of the letter. The test covers relevance, level of support, inconsistency, ignoring alternative explanations, equivocation, circularity, conditional inference, overgeneralization, and emotive language. It can be completed in fifty minutes.

As advised by Norris, freshmen were required to take a pretest the first week of the fall semester and a posttest as a small part of their final exam. To help students take the pretest seriously, they were told they were part of a large research project funded by the U.S. Department of Education, and to do their best. We also told them that because some students do worse on the posttest, the score used for the test's points on the final exam would be the higher of either the pre- or the posttest. The assessment data indicated that this approach to teaching critical thinking and writing was as good as or better than many more traditional approaches reported in the literature (Hatcher, 1999a, 1999b).

Analysis of E-W Assessment Data. For the six years in which we used the E-W, the effect size gain was +0.97 (n = 977). For comparison, we tested students in a standard logic class at a large state university and a critical-thinking class at a community college (n = 67). The effect size for the comparison groups was −0.02. This was largely because the posttest scores of the students in the standard logic class were lower than their pretest scores. As we later found out, the freshman gain of nearly a full standard deviation is quite good (Pascarella and Terenzini, 2005).

Some faculty members might be wary of using the E-W because it is an essay test and putative problems of interrater reliability as well as the time essays take to grade. However, our experience showed it is possible to achieve interrater reliability of .85 or better using bright and well-trained student graders. In addition, grading time can be reduced if researchers choose a random sample of the essays and grade only those, as opposed to grading every essay.

Assessing CT with the California Critical Thinking Skills Test. In the fall of 1996, we changed tests and began using the California Critical Thinking Skills Test (CCTST; Facione and Facione, 1994). We used the CCTST until 2004. One reason for changing was, even though interrater reliability was always relatively high, when the student grading teams changed because of graduation there was no way to tell if the scores from one pair of graders for one year were comparable to the scores given by another team the next year.

The CCTST is a popular thirty-four item multiple-choice exam that can be completed in fifty minutes. It tests many of the skills normally associated with critical thinking: interpretation, argument analysis and appraisal, deduction, logical puzzles, and induction (Facione and Facione, 1994). According to Possin (2008), the test has become quite popular, even internationally, so it is easy to compare scores with other institutions. Between 1996 and 2005, we recorded 3,234 pretest and posttest scores for 1,617 freshmen. The average gain was 2.6 points, with an effect size gain of +0.57. By comparing our gains to those cited in the literature (Hitchcock, 2004; Pascarella and Terenzini, 2005), we found that a gain of +0.57 was about average. In comparison, the mean gain for critical-thinking classes at the University of Melbourne, Monash University, McMaster University, and those used as a test validation group was +0.54 (Hitchcock, 2004).

Assessing CT with the Cornell Level Z Critical Thinking Test. In the fall of 2006, we switched to the Cornell Level Z Critical Thinking Test (Ennis, Millman, and Tomko, 2004). The CLZ is a fifty-two-question multiple-choice test that can be completed in fifty minutes. According to the test booklet, the majority of the fifty-two test items focus on deduction (seventeen) and induction (twenty-three), while the remaining items focus on observation, credibility, assumptions, and meaning (Ennis, Millman, and Tomko, 2004). One reason for the switch was, according to Fisher and Scriven (1997), "This test appears to be the most sophisticated on the market" (p. 129). Another reason was to compare our students' gains on the three standardized tests. If the difference between the effect-size gains on the E-W (0.97) and CCTST (0.57) was so large, perhaps there would also be substantial differences among the three tests. That would indeed be important (and disturbing) news for the assessment community. We have CLZ data for freshmen for three years.

Comparing the E-W, the CCTST, and the CLZ. As Table 3.1 indicates, the difference between the effect-size gain for the CCTST and the CLZ is not substantial: +0.60 and +0.57, respectively. Students gained approximately 3 percent of a standard deviation more on the CLZ than on

Table 3.1. Comparison of Effect Size Gains of the E-W, CCTST, and CLZ

BU Freshmen	Pre	St.D	Post	St.D	Diff	Mean Gain in St.D
E-W (n = 977)	7.5	5.3	12.8	5.7	5.3	0.97
CCTST (n = 1617)	15.4	4.2	18.0	4.3	2.6	0.57
CLZ (n = 369)	26.7	5.0	29.7	5.0	3.0	0.60

the CCTST. The great difference remains between the E-W (0.97) and the other two tests (mean of 0.58).

What might account for the substantial differences between the gains on the E-W and the other two CT tests? Even though the freshmen went through the same program, the difference in effect-size gains between the E-W (0.97) and both the CCTST and the CLZ (mean of 0.58) is 0.39. If educators follow the suggestion of the report from the Commission on the Future of Higher Education created by Secretary Spellings (Secretary of Education's Commission on the Future of Higher Education, 2006), which claims standardized test scores indicate the worth of a school's program and should be made public, nearly 0.40 of a standard deviation is the difference between being able to claim one's institution performs at an average level in teaching CT and performing at an uncommonly high level.

Is there something peculiar about Baker University's CT program that could explain the differences? One hypothesis is that the level of instruction in deductive and inductive logic in the Baker program, three to four weeks during the first semester, is sufficient for students to see the problems in the arguments in the E-W letter, but it is not sophisticated enough for students to do exceptionally well on the CCTST or CLZ. However, if this were so, the critical-thinking classes at McMaster and Melbourne should have done significantly better than Baker University's students because they spend an entire semester on logic, combined with computer-assisted exercises (Hitchcock, 2004; van Gelder, 2004). But their mean gains were not much higher than Baker's, so the level of understanding of logic for Baker's students must be similar to those in other programs.

A more likely explanation is, given the emphasis on the written critiques of arguments for Baker's students, the difference in format of the two kinds of tests. Writing the essay for the E-W more closely resembles what Baker's students were asked to do throughout much of the two semesters than the multiple-choice format of the CCTST or CLZ. Hence, the act of taking the E-W would seem more natural than hurriedly working through a series of tricky, multiple-choice questions found on either the CCTST or CLZ, some of which are highly artificial (Groarke, 2009). If this is so, then the E-W is a better assessment tool for students who are familiar with applying CT skills to their writing.

NEW DIRECTIONS FOR INSTITUTIONAL RESEARCH • DOI: 10.1002/ir

Implications for Assessing CT

What can institutions learn about assessment from Baker's experience with these three standardized CT tests? First, in selecting a test, as Ennis (2003) has pointed out, the faculty must choose a defensible definition of CT and the test must cover the skills entailed by that definition. It seems obvious that students will not do well on any test of material not covered in their courses. For example, if a CT program does not offer focused instruction in deductive and inductive reasoning, then tests that emphasize these skills are not appropriate. If CT instruction focuses more on informal approaches to evaluating reasoning, then a test like the E-W is a better choice. Of course, the best way to match a test to a program is to first take the test and see what it covers (Ennis, 2003).

Second, if the faculty members want to learn the specific strengths and weaknesses of their students' performance, they need to choose a test that includes error analysis. This is one of the strengths of such multiple-choice exams as the CLZ and CCTST. As Possin (2008) has pointed out in his survey and analysis of CT tests, not all tests allow error analysis. This is a problem if the results from a test are intended to yield serious feedback to teachers for making specific changes in their approaches to CT.

Third, if cost is a factor, then even though Baker's data show that students taking the CLZ and CCTST have similar effect-size gains, the cost of the two tests is not similar. The CLZ is three dollars per test booklet; if a simple answer sheet is constructed and students are instructed not to mark in the test booklets, the tests can be reused. The cost for the CCTST is seven dollars for each test taken. In more recent years, the answers to the CCTST have not been provided. Each answer sheet must be scored by its publisher, Insight Assessment, at seven dollars each. Over time, the difference in cost for these two exams is significant.

One recent and perplexing discovery with regard to Baker's assessment efforts was the range of student scores on the CLZ relative to their first-semester instructor—the semester when the logical skills covered by that test were explicitly taught. The mean gain for 369 students over the three years was +3.0 points with an effect size of +0.60, but the mean gains relative to individual instructors ranged from +6.0 to −1.0. The +6.0 gain is an effect size of +1.2, twice what would be expected, according to Pascarella and Terenzini (2005). What this shows is something we all probably know: some instructors are much better than others at teaching the logical skills needed to do well on tests such as the CLZ. Even with significant outside funding for considerable faculty development, the data indicate that some teachers were unable to teach their students the logical skills needed to do well on the CLZ.

The checkered results from the assessment also mean that one should not quickly endorse a specific approach to teaching CT based on published assessment data from one teacher teaching one section of any CT course for only one semester. For example, prior to calculating the effect-size gains relative to Baker's instructors, when Tom Solon (2003) reported effect-size gains of 0.87 on the CLZ for an experimental group of 25 students taking his Introduction to Psychology class, which included instruction in logic and CT skills, it appeared that his integrative approach was far superior to all others (Hatcher, 2006). Now, given the range of Baker's scores, such a conclusion may be unwarranted. It may just be that Solon was an excellent teacher, while others may never be able to replicate those splendid gains even if they followed his approach and used the same materials.

Finally, no matter which test one chooses to measure students' critical-thinking abilities, if one wants to compare outcomes with other similar CT programs then the easiest way to do this is to choose a widely used, standardized test appropriate to one's program and compare the outcomes with those in the literature. It does not follow that one should agree with the report from the Secretary of Education's Commission on the Future of Higher Education (2006) and endorse the use of only one standardized test, or even a small group of them, for everyone and make the results known to the public (U.S. Department of Education, 2006). There are numerous tests on the market, and they have been widely reviewed by some of the best people in the field (Ennis, 2003; Fasko, 2003; Fisher and Scriven, 1997; Norris and Ennis, 1989; Possin, 2008; Sobocan and Groarke, 2009). But, as Bob Ennis (2008) has pointed out, if only one test or a small number are used, institutions will be inclined to teach to the tests rather than a broader, richer conception of CT.

In summation, first choose or develop an adequate definition of CT, determine what skills the concept entails, and then choose a test that best assesses those skills. It is also important to consider how familiar students will be with the format of the test—that is, writing an essay versus a multiple-choice test. Given the current body of research, it is possible to know what sort of an effect-size gain should be expected with a one-semester CT course, a two-semester sequence, or freshman-to-senior gains. If the result is better than those reported in the research, this is good news (and should be shared with all). If the results are less than the norm, this is not bad; rather, it indicates that some changes should be made to address the deficiencies. That is what assessment is really about: improving student learning by finding out systematically what knowledge or skills students gain or lack by completing our programs, and then responding conscientiously to this information.

References

Bok, D. *Our Underachieving Colleges: A Candid Look at How Much Students Learn and Why They Should Be Learning More.* Princeton, N.J.: Princeton University Press, 2006.

NEW DIRECTIONS FOR INSTITUTIONAL RESEARCH • DOI: 10.1002/ir

Cederblom, J., and Paulsen, D. *Critical Reasoning* (6th ed.). Belmont, Calif.: Wadsworth, 2006.

Ennis, R. H. "Critical Thinking Assessment." In D. Fasko Jr. (ed.), *Critical Thinking and Reasoning: Current Research and Practice*. Cresskill, N.J.: Hampton Press, 2003.

Ennis, R. H. "Nationwide Testing of Critical Thinking for Higher Education." *Teaching Philosophy*, 2008, *31*, 1–26.

Ennis, R. H., Millman, J., and Tomko, T. N. *Cornell Critical Thinking Tests, Level X and Level Z Manual* (4th ed.). Seaside, Calif.: Critical Thinking, 2004.

Ennis, R. H., and Weir, E. *The Ennis-Weir Critical Thinking Essay Test*. Pacific Grove, Calif.: Midwest, 1985.

Facione, P. A., and Facione, N. C. *The California Critical Thinking Skills Test: Form A and B Test Manual*. Millbrae, Calif.: California Academic Press, 1994.

Fasko, D. (ed.). *Critical Thinking and Reasoning: Current Research, Theory, and Practice*. Cresskill, N.J.: Hampton Press, 2003.

Fisher, A., and Scriven, M. *Critical Thinking: Its Definition and Assessment*. Point Reyes, Calif.: Edgepress, 1997.

Govier, T. *The Philosophy of Argument*. Newport News, Va.: Vale Press, 1999.

Groarke, L. A. "What's Wrong with the CCTST? Critical Testing and Accountability." In J. Sobocan and L. A. Groarke (eds.), *Critical Thinking, Education and Assessment*. London, Ont.: Althouse Press, 2009.

Hatcher, D. L. "Why Formal Logic Is Essential for Critical Thinking." *Informal Logic*, 1999a, *19*(1), 77–89.

Hatcher, D. L. "Why We Should Combine Critical Thinking and Written Instruction." *Informal Logic*, 1999b, *19*(2 & 3), 171–183.

Hatcher, D. L. "Arguments for Another Definition of Critical Thinking." *INQUIRY: Critical Thinking Across the Disciplines*, 2000, *20*(1), 3–8.

Hatcher, D. L. "Stand-Alone Versus Integrated Critical Thinking Courses." *Journal of General Education*, 2006, *55*(3–4), 247–272.

Hatcher. D. L., and Spencer, L. A. *Reasoning and Writing: From Critical Thinking to Composition* (3rd ed.). Boston: American Press, 2006.

Hitchcock, D. "The Effectiveness of Computer Assisted Instruction in Critical Thinking." *Informal Logic*, 2004, *24*(3), 183–217.

Johnson, R. H. *The Rise of Informal Logic*. Newport News, Va.: Vale Press, 1996.

Johnson, R. H. *Manifest Rationality: A Pragmatic Theory of Argumentation*. Mahwah, N.J.: Erlbaum, 2000.

Johnson, R. H. "The Implications of the Dialectical Tier for Critical Thinking." In J. Sobocan and L. A. Groarke (eds.), *Critical Thinking Education and Assessment*. London, Ont.: Althouse Press, 2009.

Lipman, M. *Thinking in Education* (2nd ed.). New York: Cambridge University Press, 2006.

Mill, J. S. *On Liberty*. Indianapolis: Hackett, 1978.

Norris, S. P., and Ennis, R. H. *Evaluating Critical Thinking*. Pacific Grove, Calif.: Midwest, 1989.

Nosich, G. *Reasons and Arguments*. Belmont, Calif.: Wadsworth, 1982.

Pascarella, E. T., and Terenzini, P. T. *How College Affects Students*. Vol. 2. San Francisco: Jossey-Bass, 2005.

Possin, K. "A Guide to Critical-Thinking Assessment." *Teaching Philosophy*, 2008, *31*(3), 201–228.

Secretary of Education's Commission on the Future of Higher Education. *A Test of Leadership: Charting the Future of U.S. Higher Education*. Washington, DC: U.S. Government Printing Office, 2006.

Sobocan, J., and Groarke, L. A. (eds.). *Critical Thinking Education and Assessment*. London, Ont.: Althouse Press, 2009.

Solon, T. "Teaching Critical Thinking: The More, the Better!" *Community College Enterprise*, 2003, *9*(2), 25–38.

van Gelder, T. J., Cumming, G., and Bissett, M. "Cultivating Expertise in Informal Reasoning." *Canadian Journal of Experimental Psychology*, 2004, *58*(2), 142–152.

DONALD L. HATCHER *is professor of philosophy at Baker University and was director of its Liberal Arts Program from 1980 to 2009.*

This chapter describes recent attempts to measure context-rich application of quantitative reasoning. Initial evidence suggests that teaching to explicitly stated learning goals—whether in the context of a limited cluster of courses or in offerings across the curriculum—can shape student aptitude.

Beyond Math Skills: Measuring Quantitative Reasoning in Context

Nathan D. Grawe

In the opening paragraphs of a study sponsored by the National Council on Education and the Disciplines, Lynn Arthur Steen (2001) notes, "Unfortunately, despite years of study and life experience in an environment immersed in data, many educated adults remain functionally innumerate" (p. 1). Steen's call to action has been met by an explosion of quantitative reasoning (QR) programs. (The terms *quantitative reasoning, quantitative literacy,* and *numeracy* are used interchangeably in this literature.) A 2009 Mathematical Association of America survey of U.S. colleges found that two-thirds of institutions host a quantitative support center (see Schield, 2010). Moreover, the survey reports nearly half of institutions have developed quantitative requirements transcending the traditional math/science distribution. Clearly, much innovation has taken place.

Are these efforts effective? The first challenge in answering this question is defining the concept. Through assessing thousands of student papers and reading the theoretical literature, Carleton's Quantitative Inquiry, Reasoning, and Knowledge (QuIRK) initiative has arrived at a working definition: the habit of mind to consider both the power and limitations of quantitative evidence in the evaluation, construction, and communication of arguments in public, professional, and personal life. (See Grawe and Rutz, 2009; Lutsky, 2008; and Rutz and Grawe, 2009, for a full discussion of this definition and its implications for programming.) This definition is broad, intended to be inclusive of a range of QR conceptions. As we speak with researchers and teachers at other institutions, we have come to recognize QR as a multifaceted domain that plays out in different ways in different disciplines. A narrow definition inevitably excludes sections of the campus from the discussion—an outcome that would undermine our effort to change campus culture.

This definition contains four clear facets. First, QR requires command of mathematical skills. Students cannot appreciate the strengths and limitations of tools they do not possess. In a campus talk, Deborah Hughes Hallett (2008) suggested the necessary skills: arithmetic, percentages, graphs, estimation, elementary probability and statistics, basic geometry of measurement, and comprehension of basic growth patterns (linear vs. exponential). The absence of calculus, or even algebra, from this list is not to suggest that these tools cannot be employed by the quantitatively literate, but only that these are not essential skills. As Steen (2004) eloquently puts it, QR is "sophisticated reasoning with elementary mathematics rather than elementary reasoning with sophisticated mathematics" (p. 9).

Steen's quote points to the second facet of QR: it involves application in context (see De Lange, 2003; Steen, 2001, 2004; Richardson and McCallum, 2003; and Bok, 2006). Just as the ability to sound out words or recite grammar rules does not guarantee the comprehension and fluency of literacy, quantitative methods are not completely owned unless the student can apply them to problems in a variety of contexts.

Third, QR involves communication (see Brakke, 2003; De Lange, 2003; and Wiggins, 2003). It may be easy to see that effective communication in the twenty-first century requires facility with QR (see Rutz and Grawe, 2010; and Wolfe, 2010). With increasingly easy access to data over the internet and analysis software from basic graphics to statistical analysis tools, unsupported quantitative claims have become less and less acceptable. Max Frankel (1995) writes in the *New York Times Magazine,* "Deploying numbers skillfully is as important to communication as deploying verbs" (para. 4). Our experience at Carleton shows that even students with strong math skills may come up short in QR from inability to translate that strength into an argument. A reading of the theoretical literature foreshadows this finding.

The final facet of our definition is that QR "describes a habit of mind rather than a set of topics or a list of skills" (Hughes Hallett, 2003, p. 91). We seek to condition our students, on encountering any problem, to ask, "What do the numbers show?" The answer may be that the available quantitative evidence is misleading because it counts only the countable and not the important. Or it may be that QR does not address the question at hand. Recognition of the limitations of quantitative evidence is, after all, a key component of QR. But without what Steen (2001, p. 2) describes as the "predisposition to look at the world through mathematical eyes, to see the benefits (and risks) of thinking quantitatively about commonplace issues, and to approach complex problems with confidence in the value of careful reasoning," numeracy will be restricted to prompted course work or directed academic exercise.

NEW DIRECTIONS FOR INSTITUTIONAL RESEARCH • DOI: 10.1002/ir

Given this definition, it might be argued that quantitative and qualitative analyses are merely two alternative reflections of an overarching critical thinking. For instance, just as instructors of numeracy warn their charges to consider the construction of variables, teachers of qualitative approaches caution students to define terms. Similarly, an advocate of QR who demands students eschew "weasel words" such as *many* and *few* in place of actual figures is mimicked by the humanist demanding that pupils demonstrate precision in language. These connections may be true at an abstract level, but QR requires specific skills not usually required by generic critical thinking. For example, QR necessitates an understanding of what statistical significance means and how it is distinct from practical significance or the ability to effectively communicate information through charts and tables. It is exactly this that motivates a growing literature teaching concepts specific to thinking critically with quantitative evidence. (For examples, see Few, 2004; Miller, 2004; and Tufte, 2001.)

Direct Assessments of QR

In 2001, the National Academy of Sciences (NAS) convened a National Forum on Quantitative Literacy. Among the five major findings (summarized in Steen, 2004), the forum concluded, "QL is largely absent from our current systems of assessment and accountability" (p. 9). This is not to say there were no assessment tools. Many national surveys ask students about their comfort with, and self-assessed ability in, the use of quantitative methods. But Chun (2002), who summarizes some of the most commonly used national surveys, notes the questionable reliability of such self-reports. Chun disputes whether students understand items in the way survey constructors intended and, even if they do, whether they can or will provide accurate assessments of their own capacities. Acknowledging a viable role for such indirect assessments, Chun concludes, "If we are interested in understanding what students have learned, we should measure what students have learned" (2002, p. 25).

Wiggins (2003) argues the early lack of assessment tools was predictable, given the contextual nature of the subject and its identity as a habit of mind:

> The implications of contextualized and meaningful assessment in [QR] challenge the very conception of "test" as we understand and employ that term. Test "items" posed under standardized conditions are decontextualized by design. . . . [A]ssessment must be designed to cause questioning (not just "plug and chug" responses to arid prompts); to teach (and not just test) which ideas and performances really matter; and to demonstrate what it means to *do* mathematics [p. 125; emphasis in original].

Although traditional tests of math skills aptly measure students' ability to calculate, they obliterate demands of authentic, ill-structured problems—demands to evaluate and select evidence, choose appropriate methods, interpret results, and ask the "right" question. To contrast the nature of QR with traditional test design, six times Wiggins uses the word *messy* to describe the practice of QR.

Wiggins (2003) is undoubtedly correct in concluding that the abstract and clean environment of traditional standardized math tests cannot capture QR. However, this should not be taken to mean such assessments have no bearing on the subject. If QR requires a basic skill set, then traditional tests of students' abilities to perform calculations or comprehend graphs and tables speak to a critical facet of QR. To a degree, tests such as the SAT math exam or the CAAP mathematics subsection can serve such a purpose. Yet Steen's warning (2004) that QR values sophistication of the application over sophistication of the tool implies that scores on these mathematics exams are only proxies for aptitude in the skills required by QR. For instance, for the purposes of QR skills assessment, trigonometry and geometry play too large a role, while estimation and knowledge of basic magnitudes (such as knowing the world's population is better approximated as six billion than six trillion) is entirely overlooked.

Context-Rich Multiple-Choice Instruments. Since the 2001 NAS forum, several institutions have worked to develop alternative math skills tests that better reflect critical QR skills. Even as he noted the limitations of such tests, Steen (2004) offered sample questions to jump-start the effort. The QR program at Wellesley College (http://www.wellesley.edu/QR/) has created a full exam to identify entering students in need of skills training. Macalester College has developed a test—the Macalester Learning Assessment (MLA)—that includes multiple-choice items testing QR skills and knowledge of basic magnitudes, which they use to assess development of QR in the general education curriculum (see Bressoud, 2009, for sample items).

Of these efforts, perhaps the most developed is James Madison University's Quantitative Reasoning Test (see http://www.madisonassessment.com/view-demo for sample items). The JMU instrument is designed to evaluate student ability in two dimensions: (1) the ability to "use graphical, symbolic, and numerical methods to analyze, organize, and interpret natural phenomenon"; and (2) the capacity to "discriminate between association and causation, and identify the types of evidence used to establish causation" (Sundre, 2008, p. 4). The twenty-five-minute, multiple-choice test has been developed with large samples from JMU, including more than fourteen hundred first-year students in fall 2007 (Sundre, 2008). In that sample, both computer- and paper-based administrations proved "moderately" to "substantially" reliable (Cronbach's alpha = 0.60 and 0.65, respectively), in the terminology of Landis and Koch (1977). A spring 2008 examination of sophomores showed a slightly higher level of reliability among this more advanced student group. JMU has recently collaborated to administer the test at several other institutions, with similar success. Although the test has not yet been given to a large number of institutions, were it widely applied it could yield nationally comparable data. Readers interested in using the test should refer to its description at http://www.jmu.edu/assessment/wm_library/QR.pdf.

Alternatives to Multiple-Choice Tests. Assuming test designers can meet the challenge of incorporating the complexities of context into a multiple-choice framework, the strengths of this approach are obvious. Multiple-choice questions can assess student ability to identify the correct answer to a prescribed calculation. Moreover, students are familiar with such testing environments, scores from computer-administered tests can be calculated instantaneously, competency scores are easily calculated, and administration costs can be quite low. However, Richard Hersh (2010), co-director of the Collegiate Learning Assessment (CLA), questions whether even the best-designed test can capture the richness of complex learning outcomes such as critical thinking or quantitative reasoning. Hersh writes, "Life is not a series of multiple choice questions" (2010, p. 1). In particular, he notes the need to evaluate students' capacity "to use [their] critical thinking and analytical reasoning skills to assemble and reconcile seemingly contradictory information to deal with problems that are not easily defined" (p. 1).

Hersh's argument highlights several aspects of the working definition of QR presented above that are difficult to incorporate into any multiple-choice item. First, students must not only comprehend others' quantitative arguments in text, chart, and table; they must also be able to construct their own. Second, students must be able to discern differences in source quality. Finally, they must navigate the ambiguities of incomplete information and contradictory evidence. In Wiggins's words (2003), they must navigate the messy terrain of ill-structured, context-rich problems. This, after all, is what we do in our own work and in our lives as critical consumers and creators of arguments.

The CLA responds to these assessment challenges with a nationally comparable instrument that includes open-ended prompts with essay response. For the purposes of QR assessment, the most relevant section of the CLA is its "performance task" (see http://www.collegiatelearning assessment.org/ for a more complete discussion of the CLA, including descriptions of the analytic writing sections of the exam). Students are presented with an authentic ill-structured task. For instance, a retired prompt asks students to advise a company on its impending decision to buy an airplane for its sales staff in the wake of a crash. A "document library" offers nearly ten sources of information of varying quality that might be incorporated into brief essays, allowing students to identify and evaluate alternative perspectives. Though not all of the performance tasks involve QR, roughly 80 percent do. In asking students to construct an argument, weigh the credibility of conflicting sources, and grapple with an ill-structured problem with no clear right answer, the CLA represents an interesting counterpoint to QR-skills testing. As a national measure administered at several hundred institutions, it also produces evidence that can be used to compare student performance across campuses.

That said, the CLA's input into QR assessment is oblique at best, for two reasons. First, the creators of the instrument have intentionally taken a holistic approach that incorporates critical thinking, analytical reasoning, written communication, and problem solving. As discussed in the introduction, quantitative reasoning is a subset of this broad domain, making it difficult to interpret the scores relative to QR ability. Second, like all assessment tests, the CLA prompts students to consider particular evidence. The CLA's approach is unquestionably more open-ended than that of a traditional exam, but the presence of quantitative data at the very least prompts students to consider using that evidence in their work. Indeed, weaker students might interpret the presence of the provided data as a requirement that it be incorporated into successful responses. By contrast, authentic prompts offer no guidance as to what content should be included, leaving it up to the individual to decide what evidence should be sought. In prompting consideration of quantitative evidence, the CLA cannot discern students' habit of mind to actively seek out this information.

QR-specific open-ended, standardized prompts have been suggested by several authors. For instance, Steen (2004) and Macalester's MLA propose tests that mix multiple-choice items with brief essay prompts. Similarly, Wiggins (2003) suggests a sample instrument composed of eleven essay prompts. The MLA continues to be developed, and formal evaluation of its reliability and validity remain to be completed.

Carleton's QuIRK initiative has responded to the assessment challenge by stepping away from standardized prompts altogether, adapting writing portfolio analysis for the purpose of QR evaluation. As described in detail in Grawe, Lutsky, and Tassava (2010), QuIRK applies a QR rubric to student work drawn from the college's required sophomore writing portfolio (the rubric and associated codebook can be found at http://serc. carleton.edu/quirk/Assessment/index.html). By looking for evidence in work written for purposes other than QR assessment, we capture student behavior in the absence of a directed task. Through this approach, we can begin to assess students' habits of mind—whether or not they have been conditioned to ask "What do the numbers show?" Furthermore, many of the assignments allow students to choose their own sources. This requires them to weigh alternative pieces of evidence and consider source credibility, both key elements of numeracy in the modern world.

Rubric scorers evaluate the relevance (three categories), extent (three categories), and quality (four-point scale) of QR exhibited in the sampled paper. Extent and quality are probably clear; relevance bears some explanation. Our reading of student papers reveals two categories of QR relevance. The first is central relevance, a case in which quantitative evidence addresses a central question, issue, or theme of the work. For example, in an essay on the deterrent effect of capital punishment, QR is of central relevance.

The second category of QR relevance is peripheral relevance. QR is peripherally relevant to a paper when quantitative evidence would promote useful detail, enrich descriptions, present background, or establish frames of reference. As Miller (2004) writes, "Even for works that are not inherently quantitative, one or two numeric facts can help convey the importance or context of your topic" (p.1). For example, when introducing an argument that the combination of three philosophical definitions of poverty results in a richer conception of the condition than any one perspective alone, a student might choose to generate interest in her argument by comparing the distribution of income in the United States with that in other developed countries. QR is not at the core of this argument, and many QR-irrelevant introductions might be imagined, but the rhetorical strategy chosen by the writer calls out for quantitative evidence.

Given the potential for subjectivity among scorers, interrater reliability is a real concern with instruments of this type. Grawe, Lutsky, and Tassava (2010) report strong reader agreement in the dimensions of QR relevance and extent. Complete agreement was achieved in 75 percent and 82 percent of cases, respectively (corresponding Cohen's kappa = 0.611 and 0.693). The four-point quality scale proved slightly less reliable (perfect agreement in 67 percent of cases; kappa = 0.532), though substantial agreement was achieved when the scale was collapsed to three categories (perfect agreement in 78 percent of cases; kappa = 0.653).

The reliability of an assessment approach such as QuIRK's is undoubtedly contextual. Readers' agreement in evaluation of student work hinges on a common understanding of both the meaning of the instrument and the range of outcomes to be expected by a given student population. This claim is supported by a feasibility study conducted at Morehouse College. In reading Carleton papers, Morehouse faculty reliably applied the rubric to papers written by Morehouse students. Perfect agreement in QR quality was achieved in 82 percent of papers (kappa = 0.74). However, when those same readers scored papers written by Carleton students, reliability was notably lower, with agreement in only 52 percent of cases (kappa = 0.34). If this finding bears out in repeated study, it suggests that the QuIRK rubric can be employed effectively within a campus context but may not produce data that are comparable across institutions. Alternatively, it may mean that readers scoring works from campuses other than their own require greater training and norming to achieve useful levels of agreement.

Assessment at the Classroom, Program, and Institution Levels. Because the instruments discussed above are relatively young, most have not been thoroughly examined in a variety of contexts to formally determine their applicability. However, the details of their construction suggest some obvious limitations. QR skills assessments such as JMU's QR test have promise at all three levels of evaluation. In the case of the JMU test, reliability has been examined at the student level. Presumably, aggregations to a group of students would be more reliable still.

By contrast, the CLA and QuIRK instruments were designed for institution-level assessment. In the case of the CLA, the particular context embedded within a given performance task may not fit any one student, and so prove unreliable. In the case of the QuIRK approach, an assignment may have no QR relevance, or once again the context of an assignment may lead a student to do poorly in that specific situation. Alternatively, although the prompt may elicit QR-relevant work from one student, another student may pursue a direction for which quantitative evidence plays no role. Even in a reasonably large section, only a fraction of students may take up a QR-relevant approach, resulting in a sample size too small to analyze meaningfully. These problems are widely recognized issues pertaining to all performance-based instruments (Chun, 2002). In some sense, this is the price of authentic, highly contextualized performance tasks. For this reason, both instruments call for a large sample of students.

Fostering Improvements in Student Learning

As the citation dates seen above suggest, assessment of QR is too new to generate clear guidance as to "what works" to improve student achievement. We can, however, identify three basic approaches to QR instruction and report preliminary assessment findings. The three curricular strategies differ primarily in their breadth. The most conservative construction casts QR as a context-rich version of mathematics. A second, more expansive implementation of QR sees opportunity for instruction throughout the sciences and in some social sciences. The third and broadest conception embeds QR in courses across the curriculum, including in the traditionally less-quantitative divisions of arts, literature, and humanities.

The mathcentric approach is usually implemented in one of two ways: as "math for the liberal arts" or as statistics. Surely there is much to be gained from these mathcentric courses. Recently developed curricular materials for these types of courses constitute excellent teaching tools (see Madison and others, 2010). However, if disciplines beyond mathematics fail to engage in teaching QR, we risk sending an unintended message that QR is relevant only to mathematics. As Steen (2004) observes, "If [QR] remains the responsibility solely of mathematics departments—especially if it is caged into a single course such as 'Math for Liberal Arts'—students will continue to see it as something that happens only in the mathematics classroom" (p. 18). In addition, it seems unlikely professors in a single discipline can represent the full range of context-rich practice such as QR.

Embedding QR throughout the sciences is a large step toward greater contextual variation. JMU represents one such example. They have combined their QR test with a complementary scientific reasoning (SR) test to assess the effectiveness of the "natural world" cluster of their general education curriculum (assessment reports can be viewed at http://www. jmu.edu/assessment/JMUAssess/GenEdOverview.htm). A description of the requirement indicates that courses within the cluster explore both science and math skills and disciplinary content relevant to the study of the natural world. Not surprisingly, nearly all courses satisfying the requirement are found in the science division. JMU's assessment work reveals that student QR performance increases with the number of credit hours completed in cluster three courses and with high school advanced placement experiences that earned cluster three credits, and that QR capacity is positively related to higher grades in cluster three courses. In total, the JMU experience suggests that one effective way to increase QR skill is to require students to take courses in which professors teach to explicit QR learning outcomes.

If it is good to expose students to QR in multiple departments within a division, is it better to integrate QR throughout the curriculum? Bok (2006, p. 134) argues for this approach:

> Numeracy is not something mastered in a single course. . . . Thus quantitative material needs to permeate the curriculum, not only in the sciences but also in the social sciences and, in appropriate cases, in the humanities.

This strategy has been implemented by the QR programs at Carleton, Hollins University, Macalester College, and Wellesley College, and by the Mathematics Across the Community College Curriculum initiative.[1]

Assessment of the QR-across-the-curriculum approach has been initiated at Carleton. Because the strategy embeds QR within courses in all divisions, credit hours in the sciences serve as a poor proxy for QR exposure. Had Carleton's new QR graduation requirement been in place in the past, we might look for differences in performance by number of QR courses completed, but we will need to wait two years to be able to perform that analysis. In the meantime, longitudinal analysis lends support for the across-the-curriculum approach. Between 2005 and 2007 (just before and just after the work of the initiative began), the fraction of Carleton seniors reporting that their "use of quantitative skills is stronger or much stronger" than at college entry increased from 67 percent to 80 percent. Similarly, the fraction of graduates agreeing that QR "will be very important or essential to my life" increased from 54 percent to 68 percent. Most of this growth is due to increases among majors in the arts, literature, and humanities.

Results from QuIRK's assessment of student papers are direct evidence of success. Among papers for which QR was deemed peripherally relevant, the fraction of students employing QR has increased in five years from 28 percent to 53 percent. Similarly, the fraction of these papers rated of good QR quality rose from 9 percent to 32 percent, while the fraction rated of poor quality fell by an equal amount. A new research project examining the effects of participation in QR first-year seminars has produced promising initial results. The Carleton curricular approach to QR is less concentrated than that at JMU, but the conclusion seems to be the same: intentional teaching with attention to specific learning outcomes can improve students' QR ability.

Conclusions for Future Assessment

Despite the relative youth of QR assessment, several lessons for future assessment seem clear. First, context matters. Because QR itself is grounded in context, our assessment tools must be as well. This presents a challenge for traditional approaches to assessment, which attempt to eliminate contextual aspects of items. Nevertheless, the work at JMU and Macalester suggests it is possible to create context-rich multiple-choice items to assess QR skill competencies.

Second, no matter how carefully designed, multiple-choice exams do not capture several key aspects of the field. Students' ability to construct arguments with quantitative evidence and the habit of mind to seek out that evidence in the first place might be better assessed in essays or oral talks. The experience of the Carleton QuIRK rubric shows it is possible to develop a reliable rubric for that task.

Finally, the multifaceted nature of QR calls for a multifaceted approach to its assessment. Without directed prompts, it is impossible to test a full range of QR skills. For this purpose, the multiple-choice test is both efficient and effective. At the same time, discerning students' habits of mind requires an approach that gives students more freedom. Given this inherent tension, multiple instruments are almost surely necessary. As the educational innovations found in the Mathematical Association of America's survey mature, it will be critical to gain greater clarity as to what works in preparing students to navigate "the twenty-first century . . . world awash in numbers" (Steen, 2001, p. 1).

Note

1. Carleton: see http://serc.carleton.edu/quirk/CarletonResources/curricular_ materials.html, or http://www.mac3.amatyc.org/education/education.html. Hollins University: see http://www1.hollins.edu/homepages/hammerpw/qrhomepage. htm#applied. Macalester College: see http://www.macalester.edu/qm4pp/program/ index.html#qt. Wellesley College: see http://www.wellesley.edu/QR/overlay.htm. Mathematics Across the Community College Curriculum initiative: see http://www. mac3.amatyc.org/index.htm.

References

Bok, D. *Our Underachieving Colleges: A Candid Look at How Much Students Learn and Why They Should Be Learning More.* Princeton, N.J.: Princeton University Press, 2006.

Brakke, D. F. "Addressing Societal and Workforce Needs." In B. L. Madison and L. A. Steen (eds.), *Quantitative Literacy: Why Numeracy Matters for Schools and Colleges*. Princeton, N.J.: National Council on Education and the Disciplines, 2003.

Bressoud, D. "Establishing the Quantitative Thinking Program at Macalester." *Numeracy*, 2009, 2(1), Article 3.

Chun, M. "Looking Where the Light Is Better: A Review of the Literature on Assessing Higher Education Quality." *Peer Review*, 2002, 4(2/3), 16–25.

De Lange, J. "Mathematics for Literacy." In B. L. Madison and L. A. Steen (eds.), *Quantitative Literacy: Why Numeracy Matters for Schools and Colleges*. Princeton, N.J.: National Council on Education and the Disciplines, 2003.

Few, S. *Show Me the Numbers: Designing Tables and Graphs to Enlighten*. Oakland, Calif.: Analytics Press, 2004.

Frankel, M. "Word and Image; Innumeracy." *New York Times*, Mar. 5, 1995. Retrieved on June 11, 2010, from http://www.nytimes.com/1995/03/05/magazine/word-image-innumeracy.html?scp=1&sq=Max%20Frankel%20Innumeracy&st=cse.

Grawe, N. D., Lutsky, N. S., and Tassava, C. J. "A Rubric for Assessing Quantitative Reasoning in Written Arguments." *Numeracy*, 2010, 3(1), Article 3.

Grawe, N. D., and Rutz, C. A. "Integration with Writing Programs: A Strategy for Quantitative Reasoning Program Development." *Numeracy*, 2009, 2(2), Article 2.

Hersh, R. H. "Life Isn't a Multiple Choice Question." Retrieved on April 27, 2010, from http://www.cae.org/content/pdf/HershLifeIsntAMultipleChoiceQuestion.pdf.

Hughes Hallett, D. "The Role of Mathematics Courses in the Development of Quantitative Literacy." In B. L. Madison and L. A. Steen (eds.), *Quantitative Literacy: Why Numeracy Matters for Schools and Colleges*. Princeton, N.J.: National Council on Education and the Disciplines, 2003.

Hughes Hallett, D. "How do We Teach Quantitative Reasoning? Foster a Curricular Conspiracy." Presentation at Carleton College's Perlman Center for Teaching and Learning, Apr. 24, 2008.

James Madison University Center for Assessment and Research Studies. "Cluster Three: The Natural World Cluster Assessment Results and Interpretation." 2006. Retrieved May 12, 2010, from http://www.jmu.edu/assessment/JMUAssess/Gened/cluster_3_report_sp06.pdf.

Landis, J. R., and Koch, G. G. "The Measurement of Observer Agreement for Categorical Data." *Biometrics*, 1977, 33(1), 159–174.

Lutsky, N. S. "Arguing with Numbers: A Rationale and Suggestions for Teaching Quantitative Reasoning Through Argument and Writing." In B. L. Madison and L. A. Steen (eds.), *Calculation vs. Context: Quantitative Literacy and Its Implications for Teacher Education*. Washington, D.C.: Mathematical Association of America, 2008.

Madison, B. L., Boersma, S., Diefenderfer, C. L., and Dingman, S. W. *Case Studies for Quantitative Reasoning: A Casebook of Media Articles*. Boston: Pearson Custom Publishing, 2010.

Miller, J. E. *The Chicago Guide to Writing About Numbers*. Chicago: University of Chicago Press, 2004.

Richardson, R. M., and McCallum, W. G. "The Third R in Literacy." In B. L. Madison and L. A. Steen (eds.), *Quantitative Literacy: Why Numeracy Matters for Schools and Colleges*. Princeton, N.J.: National Council on Education and the Disciplines, 2003.

Rutz, C. A., and Grawe, N. D. "Pairing WAC and Quantitative Reasoning Through Portfolio Assessment and Faculty Development." *Across the Disciplines*, 2009, 6(Dec.). Retrieved June 11, 2010, from http://wac.colostate.edu/atd/assessment/rutz_grawe.cfm.

Schield, M. "Quantitative Graduation Requirements at US Four-Year Colleges." 2010. Retrieved on June 11, 2010, from http://statlit.org/pdf/2010SchieldJMM.pdf.

Steen, L. A. "The Case for Quantitative Literacy." In L. A. Steen (ed.), *Mathematics and Democracy: The Case for Quantitative Literacy.* Princeton, N.J.: National Council on Education and the Disciplines, 2001.

Steen, L. A. *Achieving Quantitative Literacy: An Urgent Challenge for Higher Education.* Washington, D.C.: Mathematical Association of America, 2004.

Sundre, D. L. *The Quantitative Reasoning Test*, Version 9 (QR-9), 2008. Retrieved on May 10, 2010, from http://www.madisonassessment.com/uploads/qr-9_manual_2008.pdf.

Tufte, E. R. *The Visual Display of Quantitative Information.* Cheshire, Conn.: Graphics Press, 2001.

Wiggins, G. "'Get Real!': Assessing for Quantitative Literacy." In B. L. Madison and L. A. Steen (eds.), *Quantitative Literacy: Why Numeracy Matters for Schools and Colleges.* Princeton, N.J.: National Council on Education and the Disciplines, 2003.

Wolfe, J. "Rhetorical Numbers: A Case for Quantitative Writing in the Composition Classroom." *College Composition and Communication*, 2010, *61*(3): 452–475.

NATHAN D. GRAWE *is associate professor of economics and associate dean of the college and director of the Quantitative Inquiry, Reasoning, and Knowledge (QuIRK) initiative at Carleton College.*

NEW DIRECTIONS FOR INSTITUTIONAL RESEARCH • DOI: 10.1002/ir

5

This chapter describes research on team member contributions to overall team effectiveness, and various applications of this research to developing and assessing teamwork by students on team and group projects and assignments.

Developing and Assessing College Student Teamwork Skills

Richard L. Hughes, Steven K. Jones

Astronaut Jim Lovell's words during the Apollo 13 lunar mission, "Houston, we have a problem," launched a remarkable tale of effective teamwork and creative problem solving by NASA engineers working to try to save the lives of the imperiled crew when two oxygen tanks exploded en route to the moon. Details of the dramatic and successful resolution to the problem became widely known in the motion picture *Apollo 13*, but it's not just during dramatic moments when the importance of good teamwork is needed or recognized. In fact, some form of team-oriented work is employed in most, if not all, organizations today (Hills, 2007; Kozlowski and Bell, 2003; Lawler, Mohrman, and Ledford, 1995; Morgeson, DeRue, and Karam, 2010). It would seem, then, that an important role for higher education should involve developing critical teamwork skills among students so as to prepare them for success in life.

This very point was highlighted in a 2009 poll conducted on behalf of the Association of American Colleges and Universities (AACU), in which 71 percent of employers said they wanted colleges to place greater emphasis on "teamwork skills and the ability to collaborate with others in diverse group settings" (Hart, 2010, p. 2). Many studies, in fact, have identified teamwork as one of the most valued and necessary skills among college graduates. For example, a report by the Conference Board (2008) indicated that for four-year college graduates, prospective employers rated the importance of effective teamwork and collaboration second only to oral communication in contributing to job success. This is consistent with findings from our own institutional surveys at the U.S. Air Force Academy,

NEW DIRECTIONS FOR INSTITUTIONAL RESEARCH, no. 149, Spring 2011 © Wiley Periodicals, Inc.
Published online in Wiley Online Library (wileyonlinelibrary.com) • DOI: 10.1002/ir.380

in which graduates deem teamwork "very important" to one's performance as an officer. Tellingly, the percentage of officers who endorse this view goes up as rank increases (O'Donnell, 2008). Thus, even though teamwork skills are viewed as important at all levels of employment, their importance may become increasingly evident and valued with ever-greater seniority in the organization.

It should be no surprise that teamwork was identified as one of eleven essential learning outcomes in the seminal AACU report *College Learning for the New Global Century* (National Leadership Council for Liberal Education and America's Promise, 2007). Furthermore, teamwork also plays an important *instrumental* role in education. Kuh's research (2008) shows that collaborative assignments and projects are especially potent in having a positive impact on student development. In other words, working and solving problems actively with others is not just a desirable *outcome* of student development; it is also an educational *practice* that has demonstrably high developmental impact.

The appeal of collaboration notwithstanding, the phrase *good teamwork* may seem so conceptually vague and subjective as to defy rigorous study and systematic practice. Quite a bit is known, however, about what constitutes effective teamwork, how to assess it, and how to develop it.

What Is Teamwork?

One way to answer the question "What is teamwork?" is to begin by clarifying the term *team*. Specifically, what makes a team something different from any other group of people? Teams are composed of individuals who share several defining characteristics: they (1) have a shared collective identity, (2) have common goals, (3) are interdependent in terms of their assigned tasks or outcomes, (4) have distinctive roles within the team, and (5) are part of a larger organizational context that influences their work and that they in turn can influence (Morgeson, Lindoerfer, and Loring, 2009; Kozlowski and Ilgen, 2006).

It is useful to think of these five characteristics as *dimensions* along which all groups naturally vary. Taken collectively, they are useful in distinguishing teams from certain other social collectives, such as a group of friends. On the other hand, there may not be much practical difference between a team as it is defined here and many other work groups more generally. All teams or groups vary to some extent along the five dimensions, and there is no specifiable point at which a "group" becomes a "team" (Morgeson, Lindoerfer, and Loring, 2010). Differences tend largely to be of degree rather than of nature (Guzzo and Dickson, 1996), and in many ways the terms can be used interchangeably. In academic settings, for example, it seems like splitting hairs to differentiate what may be called team projects in one course from what are called group projects in another course. What's more important than the names per se are the various structural, task, and contextual factors that influence the kinds of interactions taking place among members.

Amid this complexity, one thing seems clear: by whatever name groups or teams are known, appeals to the importance of good *teamwork* on them are common. Just what is meant by such appeals is less clear than one might think, because the term *teamwork* is inherently ambiguous and imprecise and is used in different contexts to refer to two rather distinct things. Sometimes teamwork is used to refer to *overall* team performance or effectiveness (see, for example, Goodwin and Bonadies, 2005). From this perspective, calling something "good teamwork" refers to the team's performance as a whole and to its collective success. At other times, however, the focus is on the nature and quality of *individual* team members' contributions to the team. This is clearly, for example, the aim of AACU's adoption of teamwork as one of the essential learning outcomes in a college education; it underscores the importance of developing the attitudes and skills in *individual students* necessary for contributing productively to the myriad groups and teams they'll serve on later in life. Arguably, the latter meaning of teamwork is a necessary condition for the former; you could not have effective collective teamwork without effective supporting behaviors on the part of individual team members. This does not, however, alter the fact that the level of analysis differs in the two cases.

Whereas the levels of analysis are different, the term teamwork refers in both cases to a *process* involving how team members interact more than to the team's ultimate success or the quality of its end product. This distinction is particularly important when it comes to determining ways to assess effective teamwork. Quite simply, teamwork is *not* the same thing as team success. There are many reasons a team might be successful, and not necessarily because team members worked particularly well together. A team might be successful because one member made uniquely important contributions that ensured a quality product despite marginal efforts by most team members; or a team might be successful because it was operating in a particularly munificent environment virtually guaranteeing a successful outcome; or, as in an athletic context, it may be because the opposing team played atrociously. In academic contexts, it is important to distinguish between the overall quality (say, the grade) of a group project or assignment on the one hand and the quality of each individual member's *teamwork* in contributing to that final product on the other. It may not be so uncommon, for example, that a bright and ambitious student does most of the work on a group report, earning high marks for the group while (truth be told) nonetheless exhibiting poor teamwork in producing it.

For all these reasons, as well as to avoid confusion, in this chapter we refer to teamwork primarily in its sense as a set of individual skills. Viewing teamwork as a set of skills, after all, is not the only way an individual team member's contributions to overall teamwork might be viewed. For example, team member effectiveness has also been examined in terms of personality traits such as initiative, openness, helpfulness, flexibility, and supportiveness (Kinlaw, 1991; Morgeson, Reider, and Campion, 2005; Stevens and Campion, 1994; Varney, 1989). However, because personality traits are considered to be rather enduring and resistant to change, they have been studied more for their applicability to team selection issues than as a target of developmental intervention. Our focus here on teamwork as a set of skills lays the foundation for exploring more specifically how students can acquire teamwork skills and improve their ability to use them through instruction, practice, and feedback.

This way of conceptualizing teamwork is consistent with contemporary approaches to team effectiveness, particularly those that take a functional approach. In the functional approach, team leadership is oriented around satisfaction of critical team needs and the various functions that need to be performed in order to satisfy those needs (Morgeson, DeRue, and Karam, 2010; Morgeson, Lindoerfer, and Loring, 2010; Burke and others, 2006). Illustrative team functions include defining the team mission, establishing expectations and goals, structuring and planning the team's work, sense making, monitoring work progress, and creating a supportive social climate. In this approach, all team members—not just formally appointed leaders—can play a vital role in satisfying team needs, and when they do we would say they are exhibiting good teamwork.

Therefore guidance for enhancing team effectiveness heretofore intended for formal team leaders now represents a legitimate area of contribution by other members too. Even when there are formal team leaders, multiple team members can perform many of the leaders' formal roles and functions with potentially even greater buy-in and impact. If no formal team leader is identified, knowledge of generic leadership functions can still serve as a useful template for guiding all team members' behavior in ways that enhance team effectiveness. For example, Stagl, Salas, and Burke (2007) identified a number of best practices intended to help team leaders facilitate team effectiveness. They included various practices, among them establishing a compelling direction, challenging the status quo, encouraging self-goal setting and self-observation among team members, determining team decision-making authority, establishing team norms, managing team boundaries and performance expectations, and reviewing and modifying strategies for maximizing team performance. These clearly represent functions that would enhance the effectiveness of leaderless teams, which necessarily implies that team members themselves must accept responsibility for performing them.

A final consequence of this deliberately inclusive view of team leadership is that social skills become more important in determining team members' ability to fulfill their shared responsibilities for team leadership and meeting team needs (Morgeson, DeRue, and Karam, 2010; Morgeson, Reider, and Campion, 2005; Mohrman and Cohen, 1995). Social skills reflect "interpersonal perceptiveness and the capacity to adjust one's behavior to different situational demands and to effectively influence and control the responses of others" (Ferris, Witt, and Hochwarter, 2001, p. 1076), and this kind of flexible interpersonal repertoire becomes vital in team settings, which increase interdependence among people and typically produce more work sharing, need for coordination, and greater conflict than work performed independently (Campion, Medsker, and Higgs, 1993).

In sum, we are describing teamwork as a set of skills that individuals use to foster the success of groups or teams. Some of these skills (for example, setting team goals) may be primarily cognitive in nature, while others (effectively navigating team dynamics) may be much more social. Regardless, the importance of these skills is not limited to the assigned leader of a group or team; indeed, it is important for all students to acquire teamwork skills. Consequently, we are assuming that teamwork skills can indeed be acquired as part of students' educational experiences. This seems reasonable from the fact that the AACU identified teamwork as one of the important skills to be developed during college, as well as from the record of substantial financial investments in both the government and the corporate sectors to develop teamwork skills in employees.

Assessing Teamwork

Now that we have defined *teamwork*, it is possible to identify ways to assess it in our students. Fortunately, the literature already features several attempts to assess teamwork, which we review in this section. We conclude by discussing a particularly promising practice: scoring students' teamwork skills demonstrated as they perform real work in groups or teams.

Written Teamwork Tests. One possible approach to assessing teamwork is through a written test. For example, Stevens and Campion (1994, 1999) developed a paper-and-pencil selection test for staffing work teams. Their test was designed to assess individuals' knowledge, skills, and abilities in five major areas: (1) conflict resolution, (2) collaborative problem solving, (3) communication, (4) goal setting and performance management, and (5) planning and task coordination. This was done with a thirty-five-item test in which students read brief scenarios and then chose a response from four multiple-choice alternatives. Here is a sample item from that test:

> Suppose that you find yourself in an argument with several co-workers about who should do a very disagreeable, but routine task. Which of the following would likely be the most effective way to resolve this situation? [Stevens and Campion's best answer is in italics]
>
> A. Have your supervisor decide, because this would avoid any personal bias.

B. *Arrange for a rotating schedule so everyone shares the chore.*
C. Let the workers who show up earliest choose on a first-come, first-served basis.
D. Randomly assign a person to do the task and don't change it.

A similar effort is illustrated in the work of Mumford, Van Iddekinge, Morgeson, and Campion (2008), whose Team Role Test is designed to measure respondents' knowledge of relevant team roles (see also Mumford, Campion, and Morgeson, 2006). Akin to the work described earlier, this test consists of a series of brief scenarios, followed by multiple possible responses. Test takers are asked to rate the effectiveness of each response, ranging from "very ineffective" to "very effective." A sample item from this test is shown below. This item calls for the "calibrator" role, which involves managing disputes between members of the team. An example scenario from that test is given here as well:

> You are a member of a sales team at a local bookstore, where recent sales have been decreasing substantially due to a shrinking number of customers. You are in a team meeting discussing solutions to the declining sales problem. The discussion becomes a bit heated when the oldest team member suggests that the sales numbers for the new sales reps are quite low. One of the younger reps quickly counters that every time he asks for help with a customer, the older rep takes credit for the sale. The other new sales rep simply looks at the floor and says nothing.
> Please rate the effectiveness of each of the following responses:
> 1. Get the quiet new sales rep involved by asking if she has noticed the older sales rep has taken some of her sales as well.
> 2. Remind the two sales reps that personal attacks are not appropriate and that the team should focus on the future solutions.
> 3. Support the new team members by taking their side to make sure they are not used as "scapegoats" for the team's problems.
> 4. Remind the team that making critical remarks about specific people makes people defensive and will prevent the members from accomplishing anything as a team.

The idea of a teamwork test is appealing on a number of levels. For one, paper-and-pencil tests of this sort are easy to administer and score. Furthermore, they are relatively easy to validate; respondents' scores can be correlated with other measures of team performance. Indeed, the results of both the Teamwork Test (Stevens and Campion, 1999) and the Team Role Test (Mumford, Van Iddekinge, Morgeson, and Campion, 2008) have been shown to correlate significantly with peer ratings of team performance. As such, it is possible that performance on these sorts of tests could be used as a surrogate (albeit an imperfect one) for these other ratings, which tend to be more difficult to obtain.

NEW DIRECTIONS FOR INSTITUTIONAL RESEARCH • DOI: 10.1002/ir

Despite the positive features of these paper-and-pencil tests, they may not be an ideal solution for assessing teamwork skills in our students. The principal reason is that both the Teamwork Test and the Team Role Test were designed to be selection tests for staffing work teams. As a result, each was meant to provide a snapshot of an individual's knowledge about teamwork at the time of selection. Researchers did not design these tests to be given to the same person more than once, and they did not intend the tests to be used as tools for helping students improve their teamwork skills by providing feedback about changes in those skills.

This argument is similar to one made by Wiggins (1998), who distinguished between an "audit" and what he refers to as "educative assessment." Wiggins describes an audit as something designed to check up on someone after the person's activity is over. The most obvious example would be a tax audit, which may check up on an individual's financial records after having filed the tax return. In our context, the paper-and-pencil teamwork tests described above can be considered an audit. They would presumably be administered at a single time, as a way to check up on students' knowledge and choose the highest scorers for particular tasks.

This is in contrast to educative assessment, which Wiggins (1998) describes as being in the service of educating students and improving their performance in the future. This type of assessment tends to rely on more authentic tasks where students actually demonstrate their teamwork performing real tasks. Students then receive feedback about their performance, and they can use this feedback to improve their performance the next time they try a similar task. Similarly, faculty members also use student performance as feedback about areas of strength and areas that need improvement, to guide the faculty member as she prepares students for future challenges. It is in this way that assessment can be used not just to audit student performance but also to actually enhance their learning.

Comprehensive Assessment of Team Member Effectiveness (CATME). One significant step toward Wiggins's vision of educative assessment (1998) is the Comprehensive Assessment of Team Member Effectiveness, or CATME, developed by Loughry, Ohland, and Moore (2007). The CATME consists of eighty-seven items (thirty-three on a shorter version) that load onto five factors: (1) contributing to the team's work (for example, "Did a fair share of the team's work"), (2) interacting with teammates ("Communicated effectively"), (3) keeping the team on track ("Stayed aware of fellow team members' progress"), (4) expecting quality ("Expected the team to succeed"), and (5) having relevant knowledge, skills, and abilities ("Had the skills and expertise to do excellent work"). To respond to the CATME, college students are asked to "think of a student project team that you worked on last semester. Select one member of the project team (not yourself) and evaluate that one person on all of the items in this survey." The result is a detailed set of feedback from the rater about the quality of the students' teamwork skills.

In initial testing, the CATME has been used only to measure the students' past performance. However, use of this method could potentially be expanded in a number of ways. For instance, students could be introduced to the items on the CATME at the beginning of a team project, as a way to teach them how to effectively contribute to teams. As the project went along, team members could then rate each other on their respective contributions. Conceivably, faculty members could also make observations of student teams, making independent ratings of each person's work. Those scores could then be fed back to individual students to help them improve their teamwork skills as the project continues.

Valid Assessment of Learning in Undergraduate Education (VALUE). The Association of American Colleges and Universities (Rhodes, 2010) has published rubrics for fifteen of their essential learning outcomes as part of their program Valid Assessment of Learning in Undergraduate Education (VALUE). Broadly speaking, a rubric is a scoring tool that reveals the standards by which a particular piece of work will be judged (Huba and Freed, 2000; Stevens and Levi, 2005). In the case of the AACU's teamwork rubric (available electronically at http://www.aacu.org/value/rubrics/index.cfm), the standards of performance are (1) contributes to team meetings, (2) facilitates the contributions of team members, (3) individual contributions outside of team meetings, (4) fosters constructive team climate, and (5) responds to conflict. For each of these standards, descriptions of relevant behavior are provided for four levels of performance, allowing a student's teamwork skills to be rated relatively low on one dimension but markedly higher on another.

AACU has stated that their VALUE rubrics are intended for institutional-level use, rather than for grading individual students. However, the teamwork rubric could be easily adapted to serve as a guide for students enrolled in a specific course. Then the rubric could be used in many of the same ways in which the CATME could be used: students could rate teammates on their performance, and faculty members could also rate individual students on the basis of their observations of team functioning.

Implications for Educators

The CATME and the AACU's VALUE rubric are potentially valuable tools for assessing teamwork among our students. However, implementing them successfully requires intentional effort on the part of college faculty and staff and, in many cases, requires a change to how we typically do business. In this final section, we outline what are likely to be the most significant changes.

Committing to the Development of Teamwork. Like anything else, teamwork skills are not likely to emerge spontaneously; they must be intentionally developed. Therefore, faculty members need to commit to the development of teamwork skills by going out of their way to teach students what it means to be an effective teammate, asking students to practice working in teams, and offering feedback about the development of students' teamwork skills (Bain, 2004; Fink, 2003). These may seem like obvious steps, but they are ones that may not always be taken by faculty members otherwise focused on the content of their discipline.

Making Assignments That Elicit Teamwork. To assess students' teamwork, assignments that elicit teamwork behaviors must be created (Walvoord and Anderson, 1998). This may be a change for faculty members who are accustomed to giving tests and assignments that must be completed individually. For example, an introductory engineering class at our institution asks cadets to work in teams to build a rocket—a task much different from taking an individual test or writing an individual paper. It is also possible to find teamwork opportunities outside the typical classroom setting. For instance, at our institution all of our students work in teams in field training during the summer months and, during the academic year, participate in some form of competitive athletics (intercollegiate or intramural), another venue where teamwork is regularly displayed.

Focusing on the Process. As noted earlier, a team's success or failure can occur independently of the teamwork skill of its members. This suggests that a meaningful assessment of students' teamwork skills needs to focus on the teamwork *process*, rather than on the end *product*. It is not sufficient to give students a team assignment and then score their final project (or paper, or lab report, or whatever) for its accuracy. The quality of the team process, using something like the CATME or the VALUE rubric, must also be assessed.

Providing Meaningful Feedback. Effective learning takes place when students have an opportunity to practice, receive feedback, and then try again (Bain, 2004; Fink, 2003; Wiggins, 1998). Therefore, students developing their teamwork skills must receive feedback about the quality of those skills. This feedback can reasonably come from their peers, who are most likely to see their teamwork skills in action, or from faculty members, coaches, or others who may see their teamwork in a more limited setting. Regardless of the source, feedback about student performance is necessary, meaning that faculty and staff members need to build in opportunities for it to take place. It may also be necessary to train raters on using the assessment tool. Otherwise, raters may use differing implicit definitions of effective teamwork. For example, Sexton, Thomas, and Helmreich (2000) found ratings of teamwork between nurses and physicians to be highly dependent on one's role. Seventy-seven percent of intensive care doctors reported a high level of teamwork with IC nurses, but only 40 percent of IC nurses reported high teamwork with the IC doctors.

Conclusion

In this paper, we have described teamwork as a set of important skills that can be developed in individual students. To develop those skills, we must be very clear about how teamwork is defined and how we can promote it in our students. Perhaps even more so than other outcomes described in this volume, the development of teamwork may require willingness to redesign our courses, programs, and existing assessment methodologies.

References

Bain, K. *What the Best College Teachers Do*. Cambridge, Mass.: Harvard University Press, 2004.

Burke, C. S., Stagl, K. C., Klein, C., Goodwin, G. F., Salas, E., and Halpin, S. M. "What Type of Leadership Behaviors Are Functional in Teams? A Meta-Analysis." *Leadership Quarterly*, 2006, 17, 288–307.

Campion, M. A., Medsker, G. J., and Higgs, A. C. "Relations Between Work Group Characteristics and Effectiveness: Implications for Designing Effective Work Groups." *Personnel Psychology*, 1993, 46, 823–850.

Conference Board. *New Graduates' Workforce Readiness: The Mid-Market Perspective*. 2008 (Research Report R-1413-08-RR), New York: The Conference Board, 2008.

Day, D. V., Gronn, P., and Salas, E. "Leadership in Team-Based Organizations: On the Threshold of a New Era." *Leadership Quarterly*, 2006, 17, 211–216.

Ferris, G. R., Witt, L. A., and Hochwarter, W. A. "Interaction of Social Skill and General Mental Ability on Job Performance and Salary." *Journal of Applied Psychology*, 2001, 86, 1075–1082.

Fink, L. D. *Creating Significant Learning Experiences: An Integrated Approach to Designing College Courses*. San Francisco: Jossey-Bass, 2003.

Goodwin, C., and Bonadies, M. L. "Work in Progress—Rubric for Assessing Student-led Teams: Students Speak Out." 35th ASEE/IEEE Frontiers in Education Conference, Session T4F, Indianapolis, October 19–24, 2005.

Guzzo, R. A., and Dickson, M. W. "Teams in organizations: Recent Research on Performance and Effectiveness." *Annual Review of Psychology*, 1996, 47, 307–338.

Hart Research Associates. "Raising the Bar: Employers' Views on College Learning in the Wake of the Economic Downturn." Hart Research Associates, 1724 Connecticut Avenue, NW, Washington, DC., 2009. Retrieved March 11, 2011, from http://www.aacu.org/leap/documents/2009_EmployerSurvey.pdf.

Hills, H. *Team-Based Learning*. Burlington, Vt.: Gower, 2007.

Huba, M. E., and Freed, J. E. *Learner-Centered Assessment on College Campuses: Shifting the Focus from Teaching to Learning*. Boston: Allyn and Bacon, 2000.

Kinlaw, D. C. *Developing Superior Work Teams: Building Quality and the Competitive Edge*. San Diego: Lexington Books, 1991.

Kozlowski, S., and Ilgen, D. R. "Enhancing the Effectiveness of Work Groups and Teams." *Psychological Science*, 2006, 7, 77–124.

Kozlowski, S. W. J., and Bell, B. S., "Work groups and teams in organizations." In W. C. Borman, D. R. Ilgen, and R. J. Klimoski (eds.), *Handbook of Psychology: Vol. 12. Industrial and Organizational Psychology*, London: Wiley, 2003, 333–375.

Kuh, G. *High-Impact Educational Practices: What They Are, Who Has Access to Them, and Why They Matter*. Washington, D.C.: Association of American Colleges and Universities, 2008.

Lawler, E. E., Mohrman, S. A., and Ledford, G. E. *Creating High-Performance Organizations: Practices and Results of Employee Involvement and Total Quality Management in Fortune 1000 Companies.* San Francisco: Jossey-Bass, 1995.

Loughry, M. L., Ohland, M. W., and Moore, D. D. "Development of a Theory-Based Assessment of Team Member Effectiveness." *Educational and Psychological Measurement,* 2007, *67*(3), 505–524.

Mohrman, S. A., and Cohen, S. G. "When People Get out of the Box: New Relationships, New Systems." In A. Howard (ed.), *The Changing Nature of Work.* San Francisco: Jossey-Bass, 1995.

Morgeson, F. P., DeRue, D. S., and Karam, E. P. "Leadership in Teams: A Functional Approach to Understanding Leadership Structures and Processes." *Journal of Management,* 2010, *36,* 3–39.

Morgeson, F. P., Lindoerfer, D., and Loring, D. J. "Developing Team Leadership Capability." In E. Van Velsor, C. McCauley, and M. Ruderman (eds.), *The Center for Creative Leadership Handbook of Leadership Development* (3rd ed.), San Francisco: Jossey-Bass, 2010.

Morgeson, F. P., Reider, M. H., and Campion, M. A. "Selecting Individuals in Team Settings: The Importance of Social Skills, Personality Characteristics, and Teamwork Knowledge." *Personnel Psychology,* 2005, *58,* 583–611.

Mumford, T. V., Campion, M. A., and Morgeson, F. P. "Situational Judgment in Work Teams: A Team Role Typology." In J. A. Weekley and R. E. Ployhart (eds.), *Situational Judgment Tests: Theory, Measurement, and Application.* Mahwah, N.J.: Erlbaum, 2006.

Mumford, T. V., Van Iddekinge, C. H., Morgeson, F. P., and Campion, M. A. "The Team Role Test: Development and Validation of a Team Role Knowledge Situational Judgment Test." *Journal of Applied Psychology,* 2008, *93*(2), 250–267.

National Leadership Council for Liberal Education, and America's Promise. *College Learning for the New Global Century.* Washington, D.C.: Association of American Colleges and Universities, 2007.

O'Donnell, K. *2008 USAFA Assessment of Graduates.* Report written by the U.S. Air Force Academy Office of Plans and Programs, 2008.

Rhodes, T. L. *Assessing Outcomes and Improving Achievement: Tips and Tools for Using Rubrics.* Washington, D.C.: Association of American Colleges and Universities, 2010.

Sexton, J. B., Thomas, E. J., and Helmreich, R. L. "Error, Stress, and Teamwork in Medicine and Aviation: Cross Sectional Surveys." *British Medical Journal,* Mar. 28, 2000, *320,* 745–749. Retrieved June 21, 2010, from www.bmj.com.

Stagl, K. C., Salas, E., and Burke, C. S. "Best Practices in Team Leadership: What Team Leaders Do to Facilitate Team Effectiveness." In J. A. Conger and R. E. Riggio (eds.), *The Practice of Leadership: Developing the Next Generation of Leaders.* San Francisco: Jossey-Bass, 2007.

Stevens, M. J., and Campion, M. A. "The Knowledge, Skill, and Ability Requirements for Teamwork: Implications for Human Resource Management." *Journal of Management,* 1994, *20*(2), 503–530.

Stevens, M. J., and Campion, M. A. "Staffing Work Teams: Development and Validation of a Selection Test for Teamwork Settings." *Journal of Management,* 1999, *25*(2), 207–228.

Stevens, D. D., and Levi, A. J. *Introduction to Rubrics: An Assessment Tool to Save Grading Time, Convey Effective Feedback, and Promote Student Learning.* Sterling, Va.: Stylus, 2005.

Varney, G. H. *Building Productive Teams: An Action Guide and Resource Book.* San Francisco: Jossey-Bass, 1989.

Walvoord, B. E., and Anderson, V. J. *Effective Grading: A Tool for Learning and Assessment.* San Francisco: Jossey-Bass, 1998.

Wiggins, G. *Educative Assessment: Designing Assessments to Improve Student Performance.* San Francisco: Jossey-Bass, 1998.

RICHARD L. HUGHES *is the transformation chair at the U.S. Air Force Academy, a role in which he works with senior leaders at the academy to transform its educational practices and culture to better support the academy's mission of producing leaders of character.*

STEVEN K. JONES *is the director of academic assessment at the U.S. Air Force Academy.*

NEW DIRECTIONS FOR INSTITUTIONAL RESEARCH • DOI: 10.1002/ir

Intercultural competence and related global learning outcomes are increasingly becoming a priority for postsecondary institutions to assess. This chapter discusses the complexities of assessing this outcome.

Assessing Intercultural Competence

Darla K. Deardorff

In his book *Our Underachieving Colleges*, Derek Bok (2006) laments the poor job postsecondary institutions are doing in preparing students for the twenty-first century. Other scholars have likewise noted the central responsibility of today's institutions of higher education being to train students to function more effectively in our integrated world system (Cole, Barber, and Graubard, 1994). This brings intercultural competence and diversity to the fore of what needs to be addressed within student learning. One study concluded that "the intensity of globalisation [sic] in recent years has brought intercultural competence acquisition studies back to the center [sic] stage" (Kuada, 2004, p. 10). Thus intercultural competence development is playing, and will continue to play, an ever-increasing role in the future, given the growing diversity of American society.

Given the growing importance of intercultural competence within postsecondary education, it becomes imperative to more closely examine what this concept is and how best to assess it in our students. This chapter explores definitions of intercultural competence, highlights some practices and lessons learned in the development of intercultural competence, and offers practical guidance in assessing intercultural competence.

Defining Intercultural Competence

There is no consensus on the terminology around intercultural competence (Deardorff, 2006). The terms used to refer to this concept vary by discipline (for example, those in social work use the term cultural competence, while those in engineering prefer to use global competence) and approach (the diversity field uses such terms as multicultural competence

New Directions for Institutional Research, no. 149, Spring 2011 © Wiley Periodicals, Inc.
Published online in Wiley Online Library (wileyonlinelibrary.com) • DOI: 10.1002/ir.381

and intercultural maturity). Fantini (2009) found a variety of terms being used, both within the literature and in regard to assessment tools. Among them are multiculturalism, cross-cultural adaptation, intercultural sensitivity, cultural intelligence, international communication, transcultural communication, global competence, cross-cultural awareness, and global citizenship. For the purposes of this chapter, the term used will be _intercultural competence_, given that it applies to any who interact with those from different backgrounds, regardless of location.

One of the first steps in assessment is knowing exactly what is to be assessed—in this case, in defining the concept of intercultural competence. Too often, this term is used (as are other similar terms) without a concrete definition, especially one that is grounded in the literature. As discussed by Fantini (2009), it is essential to arrive at a definition of intercultural competence before proceeding with any further assessment endeavors. In defining intercultural competence, it is important to recognize that scholars have invested effort for more than five decades in developing this concept within the United States, and individuals should consider this body of research when proposing a working definition of intercultural competence. However, two studies (Deardorff, 2006; Hunter, White, and Godbey, 2006) showed that in the case of postsecondary institutions such definitions and scholarly work were often not used; instead, definitions relied primarily on faculty discussion, without any consultation of the literature.

There are countless definitions and frameworks published on intercultural competence. The first study to document consensus among leading intercultural experts, primarily from the United States, on aspects of intercultural competence (Deardorff, 2006) was determined through a research methodology called the Delphi technique, an iterative process used to achieve consensus among a panel of experts. The aspects on which these experts reached consensus were categorized and placed into a model (Figure 6.1) that lends itself to assessment and to further development of detailed measurable learning outcomes. Specifically, this model was derived from the need to assess this nebulous concept; hence its focus on internal and external outcomes of intercultural competence based on development of specific attitudes, knowledge, and skills inherent in intercultural competence.

Given that the items within these dimensions are still broad, each aspect can be developed into more specific measurable outcomes and corresponding indicators depending on the context. The overall external outcome of intercultural competence is defined as _effective_ and _appropriate_ behavior and communication in intercultural situations, which again can be further detailed in terms of indicators of appropriate behavior in specific contexts.

There are several key points to consider in this grounded-theory-based model that have implications for assessment of intercultural

Figure 6.1. Intercultural Competence Model

INTERCULTURAL COMPETENCE MODEL

From "The Identification and Assessment of Intercultural Competence as a Student Outcome of Internationalization at Institutions of Higher Education in the United States" in Journal of Studies in International Education, Fall 2006, 10, pp. 241–266 and in The SAGE Handbook of Intercultural Competence, 2009 (Thousand Oaks, Calif.: Sage).

Process Model of Intercultural Competence (Deardorff, 2006, 2009):

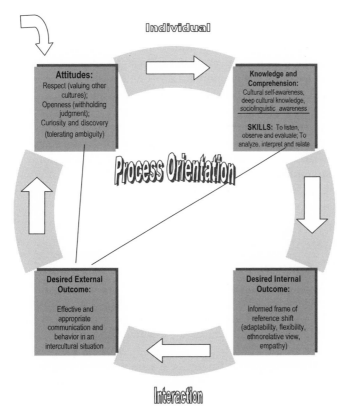

Notes:

- *Begin with attitudes; move from individual level (attitudes) to interaction level (outcomes)*
- *Degree of intercultural competence depends on acquired degree of attitudes, knowledge/comprehension, and skills*   **Copyright 2006 by D.K. Deardorff**

competence. First, intercultural competence development is an ongoing process, and thus it becomes important for individuals to be given opportunities to reflect on and assess the development of their own intercultural competence over time. In addition, this suggests assessment should be integrated throughout targeted interventions.

Second, critical-thinking skills play a crucial role (see the Skills module in Figure 6.1) in an individual's ability to acquire and evaluate knowledge. This means that critical-thinking assessment could also be an appropriate part of intercultural competence assessment.

Third, attitudes—particularly respect (which is manifested variously in cultures), openness, and curiosity—serve as the basis of this model and have an impact on all other aspects of intercultural competence. Addressing attitudinal assessment, then, becomes an important consideration.

Fourth, intercultural experts agreed on only one aspect of this study: the ability to see from others' perspectives. As a result, assessing global perspectives and the ability to understand other worldviews becomes an important consideration as well. This deep cultural knowledge entails a more holistic, contextual understanding of a culture, including the historical, political, and social contexts. Thus any assessment of culture-specific knowledge needs to go beyond the conventional surface-level knowledge of foods, greetings, customs, and so on. Further, knowledge alone is not sufficient for intercultural competence development; as Bok (2006) indicated, developing skills for thinking interculturally becomes more important than actual knowledge acquired.

Models of Intercultural Competence

There are other models that have been used to frame aspects of intercultural competence, among them Bennett's Developmental Model of Intercultural Sensitivity (1993), King and Baxter Magolda's intercultural maturity model (2005), and Cross's cross-cultural continuum (1988), all of which are developmental in nature, meaning they outline stages of growth. There are other models and frameworks purporting to define intercultural competence (see Spitzberg and Changnon, 2009, for a more thorough discussion), although many are not based on actual research. Regardless, in assessing intercultural competence, it becomes very important to define this concept within the context in which it will be used; to that end, frameworks such as the ones highlighted here can become a key tool in laying the groundwork for assessing intercultural competence. These intercultural competence models can help educators specifically identify characteristics of intercultural competence that can be prioritized and translated into clear learning objectives that are actually measured or evaluated through assessment plans.

Practices That Lead to Development of Intercultural Competence. How can intercultural competence be developed in students?

There are two means by which this can be done in postsecondary education: through the curriculum, and through co-curricular activities. This is often termed "internationalizing" the campus, which means bringing an intercultural and global dimension to students' educational experiences.

Data show that fewer than 10 percent of undergraduates take a course in international relations, and fewer than 20 percent of four-year colleges even require more than two years of foreign language study (Bok, 2006). It is thus incumbent on postsecondary institutions to ensure that intercultural competence is integrated throughout undergraduates' course work.

What does it mean to infuse intercultural competence and global learning into courses? First, it is important to understand what it is *not*, which may often be relegated to inclusion of an international reading in a course or addressing this topic in one lecture, or even taking just one course in international studies or a related topic. Such cursory treatment is far too limited in guiding students through the developmental process of intercultural competence acquisition. To that end, intercultural competence needs to be addressed throughout many undergraduate courses, in particular STEM courses (science, technology, engineering, and mathematics), and faculty themselves need to understand more fully this concept as they integrate it into the curriculum. This infusion of intercultural competence and global learning into courses entails finding multiple ways throughout a course to bring in diverse perspectives on issues, helping students begin to see from multiple cultural perspectives, using students' diverse backgrounds within a course, and requiring students to have either a local cultural immersion or an education abroad experience (possibly through research, service learning, or internship, in addition to study) related to the major.

Given that intercultural competence manifests differently depending on the discipline, it becomes important for academic departments to engage in reflection and collaboration around a number of questions: What intercultural skills and knowledge are needed in this major? How does globalization affect this major, and what global learning should be required of graduates of this major? How can departmental assessments of students' intercultural competence go beyond one aspect, such as knowledge, to ensure that students have actually attained a degree of intercultural competence, and what will be the evidence of this? How can we prepare our students to comprehend the multitude of countries and cultures that may have an impact on their lives and careers? More broadly, what knowledge, skills, and attitudes do our students need if they are to be successful in the twenty-first century? Bok (2006) outlines how colleges can better equip students for a more global, interdependent world, notably the requirement of a well-constructed foundational course that provides a framework for understanding a variety of perspectives on global issues, including foreign and comparative material into courses, and requiring foreign language.

Beyond integration of intercultural competence outcomes within courses, it is important to understand that intercultural learning is transformational learning, which requires experiences (often beyond the classroom) that lead to this transformation. Consequently, development of intercultural competence does not unfortunately "just happen" through learning about another culture or because persons from differing backgrounds are in the vicinity of one another, or even interacting with each other (Allport, 1954). To this end, service learning and education abroad become two mechanisms by which students' intercultural competence can be further developed, leading to students' transformation (see Deardorff and Edwards, forthcoming).

Intercultural interaction is central to both service learning and education abroad experiences. The contact hypothesis theory (Allport, 1954) constitutes a helpful foundation on which to implement intercultural experiences successfully. Erickson and O'Connor (2000) claim that "contact theory . . . was introduced and developed by social psychologists to examine and evaluate the various conditions under which face-to-face contact would promote greater personal and social understanding between members of different ethnic and racial groups" (p. 63). Among those conditions for optimal learning interactions are common goals, intergroup cooperation, equal status of interactants, and mutual support for rules, laws, customs, and authorities.

Service Learning. Assessment of intercultural competency within service learning is often conducted in international service-learning settings (see Camacho, 2004; Kiely, 2004; Merrill and Pusch, 2007; Parker and Dautoff, 2007; Urraca, Ledoux, and Harris, 2009). Although it is identified and assessed as intercultural competence in some domestic service learning settings (see Fitch, 2004, 2005; Slimbach, 1996), more often research on domestic service learning has referred to such assessment in terms of cultural responsiveness (Brown and Howard, 2005), multicultural learning (Boyle-Baise, 2002; Paoletti, Segal, and Totino, 2007), or diversity (Baldwin, Buchanan, and Rudisill, 2007). Even though cultural responsiveness, multicultural learning, and diversity share similarities with intercultural competence, domestic and international service learning would benefit from using the structure(s) within intercultural competence theories to more intentionally frame articulation of learning objectives, project planning, community engagement, and critical reflection in order to more clearly express specific characteristics for assessment and move away from discussing the learning that is occurring in broad terms.

By its very nature, service learning "involve[s] students in relationships across human differences, e.g. gender, race, age, economic status, national origin, faith, sexual [and gender orientations], and/or educational attainment" (Slimbach, 1996, p. 102). These intercultural exchanges mean that some learning about identities different from students' own will occur; the question becomes, Will the learning perpetuate stereotypes or will it open students to be more appropriate and effective in their views about and engagement with other people, especially those who differ from them? Assessment through critical reflection can help ascertain the degree to which students learn and understand their own and others' identities, which is an important element in intercultural competence development.

Education Abroad. Assessment with education abroad usually involves pretesting and posttesting, along with a program satisfaction survey. Recently, though, an increasing number of study abroad programs are more intentionally addressing intercultural learning and incorporating assessment throughout the program (Vande Berg and Paige, 2009). Study abroad assessments often include a self-perspective inventory, along with direct evidence of student learning such as critical reflection papers, others' observations of students' interactions, and capstone projects.

A fundamental aspect of study abroad programs (as well as service learning opportunities) is adequate preparation of students in intercultural learning so that they are better able to articulate the learning that occurs, beyond declaring that it "changed my life." This adequate preparation means helping students with an understanding of intercultural competence frameworks, vocabulary, and concepts so that they can apply them to the learning that occurs before, during, and after the experience.

On Campus. Given the small percentage of American college students who study overseas, it is crucial for institutions to maximize the curricular and co-curricular resources available on every campus, from international students and scholars to international faculty, to service learning opportunities in the community—something that has been referred to as "internationalization at home" or IaH (Nilsson, 2003). This integrated approach to programming, within a larger campus internationalization context, can help institutions develop more comprehensive programming that goes beyond fostering social opportunities to actually creating intercultural learning opportunities for all students. Maximization of such resources and opportunities is essential in development of all students' intercultural competence in preparing them for the twenty-first century.

Programming that brings together international and domestic students in intentional ways is one mechanism to help further students' intercultural competence. As Bok (2006) notes, "The best way for undergraduates to learn from one another is not through taking classes but in the dorm room discussions, mealtime conversations, and other group activities" on campus (p. 248). Placing the programming within the context of comprehensive institutional internationalization efforts through an integrated "internationalization at home" approach can benefit both students and the institution.

Given that the only element all the experts agreed on in the Deardorff (2006) study was the importance of being able to understand and see the world from others' perspectives, it becomes important for programs, whenever possible, to address multiple worldviews and comparative perspectives. For example, speaker series that bring in people from diverse backgrounds can raise awareness of other perspectives on specific issues. Likewise, foreign films become a way to bring in other worldviews, especially if combined with discussion and reflective work.

There is also a great need for programs to bring domestic and international students together in *meaningful* interactions. Such programs would involve adequately preparing (such as during orientation or through cross-cultural training) for interaction between domestic and international students, having specific intercultural learning goals for all participants, and encouraging meaningful domestic-international interactions through relationship-building opportunities. These opportunities could take the form of programs such as community service, mentoring, language partnering, book clubs, and even intramural sports.

Assessment Process for Intercultural Competence

Prioritizing Goals Related to Intercultural Competence. As discussed earlier in this chapter, the important first step in assessing intercultural competence is to define the concept itself by using the existing literature and work as a basis for the definition and framework. Most definitions and models tend to be somewhat general in terminology, so once a definition has been determined, it is important to develop a process that generates specific measurable outcomes and indicators within the context to be assessed.

To begin this process, it is best to prioritize specific aspects of intercultural competence based on the overall mission, goals, and purpose of the course or program. The definition used for intercultural competence will determine both the aspects to be assessed and the level of assessment (individual, program, organization). As in the case of learning outcomes, the level is usually that of the individual and the learning that occurs for each individual. For example, from the overall mission, "understanding others' perspectives" may be an essential aspect of intercultural competence to assess and thus become a stated goal. From that point, one would engage other key persons in dialogue about the specific measurable outcomes related to this overall goal as to the best ways to achieve it. These ways of achieving the stated goal become the specified objectives (which will be discussed in more detail shortly).

The process of prioritizing various aspects of intercultural competence is an important one and should not be done too quickly or taken lightly. The process itself often involves dialogue and discussion with key stakeholders, including students, to determine which specific elements of intercultural competence should be the focus of programmatic efforts and assessment endeavors. It is important that prioritization not be a one-time discussion but rather an ongoing process since priorities may change from program to program, from course to course, or from year to year. Generally, it is advisable to choose two or three specific aspects to assess at a given time, to control the amount of time, effort, and resources needed in the assessment efforts.

Stating Goals and Measurable Objectives. It is very important to spend sufficient time defining intercultural competence and developing clear, realistic, and measurable learning outcome statements based on the goals and prioritized foci of intercultural competence aspects (instead of the concept as a whole) because these outcome statements determine the assessment methods and tools to be used. Already developed frameworks of intercultural competence, as previously discussed, can be used in framing and defining this concept. Once the specific aspects of intercultural competence have been prioritized, it is time to write measurable objectives, or outcomes statements, related to each of the prioritized aspects (see Chapter Two of this volume).

A key part of assessment is to ensure identification of realistic objectives: can they be accomplished within the parameters of the course or program? Are these objectives specifically addressed in the program or curriculum? For example, it would not be realistic to expect a participant at a beginning language level to speak another language fluently after only two or three weeks in another country. Likewise, for short-term study-abroad programs in postsecondary institutions, outcomes must realistically match the length and learning interventions of the program.

The American Council on Education (2007a) lists common intercultural learning outcomes found at the intersection of international and multicultural education. Even these statements can be tailored more specifically to a particular course or discipline. Another resource to use for outcomes statements is the intercultural rubric developed by faculty through the American Association of Colleges and Universities (AACU, http://www.aacu.org/value/rubrics/).

Given the complexity of intercultural competence, a multimethod, multiperspective assessment plan is desired. Advocating use of multiple measures in assessing competence, Pottinger (1979) stresses that "how one defines the domain of competence will greatly affect one's choice of measurement procedures" (p. 30) and notes that pen-and-paper assessment tests have been widely criticized, in part because of the effect of the test format and also the limits a paper test places on the complex phenomena being measured. Since competence varies by setting, context, and individual, using a variety of assessments (see Chapter Two), both direct and indirect, ensures stronger measurement.

Further, using the definition of "effective and appropriate behavior and communication in intercultural settings" (Deardorff, 2006), measures need to have multiple perspectives, beyond the learner's. The learner can indicate to what degree he or she has been effective in an intercultural setting, but it is only the other person who can determine the appropriateness of behavior and communication in the interaction.

So, what does this all mean in assessing intercultural competence? Such assessment involves effort, and there is unfortunately no silver bullet regarding an assessment tool; given the complexity of this concept, it would be challenging—if not impossible—for one tool to measure an individual's intercultural competence. For example, there are numerous questions to answer: "Intercultural competence from whose perspective, and according to whom?" and "Intercultural competence to what degree?" Further, specific priorities of intercultural competence for a course, department, or institution will vary as determined by each unit's unique mission statement and goals. Thus the tool being used in one course or program may not be appropriate for another course or program if the goals differ.

Given how daunting intercultural competence assessment can seem, it is important to start with manageable portions. This means starting with one or two clearly stated intercultural competence learning outcomes. Then, design an assessment package around those outcomes that consists of one direct measure and one indirect measure. To collect this evidence, it is helpful to explore what is already being done to collect evidence of student learning and simply adapt data already being collected so that the data align with the stated outcomes. This may involve adding a couple of questions on an institutional survey to students, or on a study-abroad satisfaction survey. Or it could mean using data already collected, such as through the National Survey of Student Engagement (NSSE).

Assessment Approaches, Methods, and Tools. As just discussed, it is important that a combination of direct and indirect evidence be collected to assess students' intercultural competence, given its complexity. Here are some brief descriptions of approaches that can be incorporated into an assessment plan.

Direct Evidence: Learning Contracts. When appropriate, it is often helpful to work with learners to have them develop their own learning objectives related to the overall intercultural competence goals. This not only ensures a more effective and relevant learning process but also allows the learner to indicate the evidence for successful learning. Learning contracts consist of the learner negotiating with the instructor on what specifically will be learned, how it will be learned, the time line for learning to occur, evidence of learning, and action taken as a result of the learning. (See Malcolm Knowles, 1975, for further details on learning contracts.)

Direct Evidence: E-portfolios. Many institutions are turning to e-portfolios as a means of collecting direct evidence of students' intercultural or global learning. Artifacts placed in the portfolios by students include reflection papers, term papers, photos, and other documentation of student learning. Numerous software programs support e-portfolio development and track specific learning outcomes. Assessment of port-folios is often implemented with rubrics. Rubrics for intercultural compe-tence, and several other areas, were developed with faculty across the United States over an eighteen-month period by the AACU.

Direct Evidence: Critical Reflection. Reflection is essential in devel-oping learners' intercultural competence (Deardorff, 2006). Thus journal-ing, blogging, and reflection papers become tools through which to collect data on student learning. One tool to use in pushing students to go beyond descriptive reflection is to use a set of *what* questions: What? So what? Now what? Or simply ask students, "As a result of this learning, what will you do now?" (Knefelkamp, 1989) Writing prompts can also be used: "I learned that. . . . This is important because. . . . As a result of this learning, I will . . ." (Clayton, 2010).

Reflection should be thought of as a critical and legitimate process for promoting and assessing learning. Well-designed reflection goes beyond journal writing (although this may be an aspect of it); it is an "intentional, structured, and directed process that facilitates exploration for deeper, contextualized meaning linked to learning outcomes" (Rice and Pollack, 2000, p. 124). Through effective reflection, students can engage in an examination of their personal opinions, attitudes, and positionalities; explore their relation to others and the work in which they are engaged; and bridge their day-to-day interactions with individuals to broader social and cultural issues (O'Grady, 2000; Rice and Pollack, 2000). Such reflec-tion can be a rich source of data for research on students' intercultural competence development within the curricular context and, when com-bined with other data sources and methods, help inform creation of a more rigorous assessment plan.

Direct Evidence: Performance. Increasingly, observation of stu-dents' performance in intercultural situations is becoming a way in which to obtain others' perspectives regarding the appropriateness of students' behavior and communication. For example, a host family may be asked to complete a reflection on a student homestay. Supervising teachers may be asked to complete observations of student teachers' interactions in the classroom. Supervisors may be asked to do the same for interns, and so on. Such performance assessment is an opportunity for students to apply intercultural knowledge and skills in relevant contexts.

Indirect Evidence. Indirect evidence of student learning around intercultural competence is collected primarily through surveys or inven-tories from the learner-perspective. There are more than one hundred such instruments currently available, some with more evidence of reliability and validity than others (see Fantini, 2009). In employing these instru-ments, it is absolutely critical that users understand exactly what the instrument measures and how this aligns with the stated learning out-come. It is also very important that use of any of these indirect measures be coupled with direct measures of student learning, as discussed earlier.

In selecting indirect intercultural assessment tools, some key questions can aid in selecting the most appropriate tool(s): What are the goals and objectives to be assessed? What evidence is needed to indicate success at achieving these objectives? What does the tool measure? How well does the tool align with the stated objectives? What are the limitations and cultural biases of the tool? Is the tool valid (accurate) and reliable (consistent)? Is there a theoretical foundation for the tool? Does the tool measure human development relevant to intercultural competence? Are the administrative and logistical issues involved manageable? How will the data be used to provide feedback to students on their own intercultural competence development? (For further detail on intercultural competence assessment, see Bolen, 2007; Deardorff, 2009; Fantini, 2009; Paige, 2004; and Stuart, 2009).

Other indirect evidence related to students' perceptions of intercultural learning and intercultural competence development can be collected through interviews and focus groups.

Some Examples of Intercultural Competence Assessment. Given challenges to assessing intercultural competence, are there examples of programs that are indeed engaged in such assessment? International education programs in postsecondary institutions offer some illustrations. Georgia Tech uses a self-perspective inventory, a portfolio, and a capstone course to assess intercultural learning. Another example is Duke University, which uses several self-perspective inventories, combined with self-reflection assignments, observations, and embedded course assessments. On a broader scale, the American Council on Education (2007b) has worked with numerous institutions within the United States in articulating global learning outcomes. Through this process, multiple assessments were used, primarily through an e-portfolio method and a custom-developed self-report instrument.

Other postsecondary institutions have also engaged in assessing intercultural competence through multiple measures, among them use of self-perspective, journals, host family observations, supervisor observations, faculty observations, embedded in-class assignments, participant interviews, focus groups, and portfolios. It was not unusual for these programs to spend months—and in some cases up to two years—articulating the initial goals and objectives for developing and implementing an assessment plan on intercultural competence and global learning.

Conclusion

Assessing intercultural competence as a learning outcome is not only possible but also necessary as postsecondary institutions seek to graduate global-ready students. Given the complexity of assessing intercultural competence, other questions can be raised: How do educators avoid oversimplification of intercultural competence and yet develop reliable methods with which to measure student outcomes of internationalization? How can educators avoid the inherent limits of assessment methods (such as those associated with tests, inventories, and self-report instruments)? How can assessment of intercultural competence be integrated throughout a student's postsecondary experience? Should intercultural competence be assessed generally, or specifically? What constitutes core intercultural competence? Is identification of components of core intercultural competence too simplistic? What roles do personal traits, self-schema, emotions, and motives play in intercultural competence development and assessment? How can intercultural competence be assessed as a "social judgment" made by persons involved in the interaction (Lustig and Koester, 2006)?

This plethora of questions points to the need for additional research on assessment of intercultural competence. In the meantime, however, current research as discussed in this chapter suggests that intercultural competence assessment begins with a clear definition and framework derived from the literature, which translates into concrete, specific goals and measurable student learning outcomes. These prioritized learning outcomes are then assessed through both direct and indirect measures.

Ultimately, assessment and learning are integral to student development and thus assessment goes beyond simply documenting students' overseas experiences or international courses completed. Rather, what is the evidence that students are developing intercultural competence? Educators need to use the assessment data to guide students in their development as well as to look more broadly at the collective impact institutions have on student learning in answering the question, "How well prepared are our students for this global world in which we live and work?"

References

Allport, G. *The Nature of Prejudice.* Reading, Mass.: Addison-Wesley, 1954, 1979.

American Council on Education. "Toolkit: International Learning Outcomes." 2007a. http://www.acenet.edu/Content/NavigationMenu/ProgramsServices/cii/res/assess/intl_learn_Outcomes.htm#lessons.

American Council on Education. "Web Guide: Assessing International Learning Outcomes." 2007b. http://www.acenet.edu/Content/NavigationMenu/ProgramsServices/cii/res/assess/index.htm.

Baldwin, S. C., Buchanan, A. M., and Rudisill, M. E. "What Teacher Candidates Learned About Diversity, Social Justice, and Themselves from Service-Learning Experiences." *Journal of Teacher Education,* 2007, *58*(4), 315–327.

Bennett, M. J. "Towards Ethnorelativism: A Developmental Model of Intercultural Sensitivity." In R. M. Paige (ed.), *Education for the Intercultural Experience.* Yarmouth, Me.: Intercultural Press, 1993.

Bok, D. *Our Underachieving Colleges: A Candid Look at How Much Students Learn and Why They Should Be Learning More.* Princeton: Princeton University Press, 2006.

Bolen, M. (ed.). *A Guide to Outcomes Assessment in Study Abroad.* Carlisle, Pa.: Forum on Education Abroad, 2007.

Boyle-Baise, M. *Multicultural Service Learning: Educating Teachers in Diverse Communities.* New York: Teachers College Press, 2002.

Brown, E., and Howard, B. "Becoming Culturally Responsive Teachers Through Service-Learning: A Case Study of Five Novice Classroom Teachers." *Multicultural Education,* 2005, *12,* 2–8.

Camacho, M. "Power and Privilege: Community Service Learning in Tijuana." *Michigan Journal of Community Service Learning,* 2004, *10,* 31–42.

Clayton, P. "Generating, Deepening, and Documenting Learning in Experiential Education: The Power of Critical Reflection." (Presentation.) Ryerson University, Toronto, Ontario, March, 2010.

Cole, J. R., Barber, E. G., and Graubard, S. R. (eds.). *The Research University in a Time of Discontent.* Baltimore, Md., and London: John Hopkins University Press, 1994.

Cross, T. "Cross-Cultural Continuum for Agencies and Individuals." 1988. http://www.cfilc.org/atf/cf/%7BFF5A65B0-F157-496A-80B2-D0F5B1AE44C2%7D/CULTURAL%20AND%20DISABILITY%20COMPETENCE%20CONTINUUM.ppt.

Deardorff, D., and Edwards, K. "Assessing Intercultural Competence in Service Learning." In P. H. Clayton, R. G. Bringle, and J. A. Hatcher (eds.), *Research on Service Learning: Conceptual Frameworks and Assessment.* Sterling, Va: Stylus, forthcoming.

Deardorff, D. K. "The Identification and Assessment of Intercultural Competence as a Student Outcome of Internationalization at Institutions of Higher Education in the United States." *Journal of Studies in International Education,* 2006, *10*(3), 241–266.

Deardorff, D. K. (ed.). *The SAGE Handbook of Intercultural Competence.* Thousand Oaks, Calif.: Sage, 2009.

Erickson, J. A., and O'Connor, S. E. "Service-Learning: Does It Promote or Reduce Prejudice?" In C. R. O'Grady (ed.), *Integrating Service Learning and Multicultural Education in Colleges and Universities.* Mahwah, N.J.: Erlbaum, 2000.

Fantini, A. "Assessing Intercultural Competence: Issues and Tools. In D. K. Deardorff (ed.), *The SAGE Handbook of Intercultural Competence.* Thousand Oaks, Calif.: Sage, 2009.

Fitch, P. "Effects of Intercultural Service-Learning Experiences on Intellectual Development and Intercultural Awareness." In S. H. Billig and M. Welch (eds.), *New Perspectives in Service-Learning: Research to Advance the Field.* Greenwich, Conn.: Information Age, 2004.

Fitch, P. "In Their Own Voices: A Mixed Methods Approach to Studying of Intercultural Service-Learning with College Students." In S. Root, J. Callahan, and S. H. Billig (eds.), *Improving Service-Learning Practice: Research on Models to Enhance Impacts.* Greenwich, Conn.: Information Age, 2005.

Hunter, W., White, G., and Godbey, G. "What Does It Mean to Be Globally Competent?" *Journal of Studies in International Education,* Fall 2006, *10,* 267–285.

Kiely, R. "A Chameleon with a Complex: Searching for Transformation in International Service-Learning." *Michigan Journal of Community Service Learning,* 2004, *10,* 5–20.

King, P. M., and Baxter Magolda, M. B. "A Developmental Model of Intercultural Maturity." *Journal of College Student Development,* 2005, *46*(6), 571–592.

Knefelkamp, L. "Assessment as Transformation." Speech at American Association for Higher Education Fourth National Conference on Assessment in Higher Education, Atlanta, June, 1989.

Knowles, M. S. *Self-Directed Learning: A Guide for Learners and Teachers.* Upper Saddle River, N.J.: Prentice Hall/Cambridge, 1975.

Kuada, J. "Intercultural Competence Development of Danish Managers." 2004. Retrieved Apr. 12, 2004, from http://www.business.aau.dk/ivo/publications/working/wp33.pdf.

Lustig, M. W., and Koester, J. *Intercultural Competence: Interpersonal Communication Across Cultures.* Boston: Pearson, 2006.

Merrill, M., and Pusch, M. "Apples, Oranges, and Kumys: Models for Research on Students Doing Intercultural Service Learning." In S. B. Gelmon and S. H. Billig (eds.), *From Passion to Objectivity: International and Cross-Disciplinary Perspectives on Service Learning research.* Greenwich, Conn.: Information Age, 2007.

Nilsson, B. "Internationalisation at Home from a Swedish Perspective: The Case of Malmö." *Journal of Studies in International Education,* 2003, 7(1), 27–40.

O'Grady, C. *Transforming the Classroom, Transforming the World: The Integration of Service Learning and Multicultural Education in Higher Education.* Mahwah, N.J.: Erlbaum, 2000.

Paige, R. M. "Instrumentation in Intercultural Training." In D. Landis, J. M. Bennett, and M. J. Bennett (eds.), *Handbook of Intercultural Training* (3rd ed.). Thousand Oaks, Calif.: Sage, 2004.

Paoletti, J. B., Segal, E., and Totino, C. "Acts of Diversity: Assessing the Impact of Service-Learning." In *Scholarship of Multicultural Teaching and Learning* (Special Issue.) New Directions for Teaching and Learning, no. 111, 2007.

Parker, B., and Dautoff, D. "Service-Learning and Study Abroad: Synergistic Learning Opportunities." *Michigan Journal of Community Service Learning,* 2007, *13,* 40–53.

Pottinger, P. S. "Competence Assessment: Comments on Current Practices." In P. S. Pottinger and J. Goldsmith (eds.), *Defining and Measuring Competence.* San Francisco: Jossey-Bass, 1979.

Rice, K., and Pollack, S. "Developing a Critical Pedagogy of Service Learning: Preparing Self-Reflective, Culturally Aware and Responsive Community Participants." In C. O'Grady (ed.), *Transforming the Classroom, Transforming the World: The Integration of Service Learning and Multicultural Education in Higher Education.* Mahwah, N.J.: Erlbaum, 2000.

Slimbach, R. "Connecting Head, Heart, and Hands: Developing Intercultural Service Competence." In R. Sigmon (ed.), *Journey to Service-Learning: Experiences from Independent Liberal Arts Colleges and Universities.* Washington, D.C.: Council of Independent Colleges, 1996.

Spitzberg, B., and Changnon, G. "Conceptualizing Intercultural Competence." In D. K. Deardorff (ed.), *The SAGE Handbook of Intercultural Competence.* Thousand Oaks, Calif.: Sage, 2009.

Stuart, D. K. "Assessment Instruments for the Global Workforce." In M. Moodian (ed.), *Contemporary Leadership and Intercultural Competence: Exploring the Cross-Cultural Dynamics Within Organizations.* Thousand Oaks, Calif.: Sage, 2009.

Urraca, B., Ledoux, M., and Harris, J. "Beyond the Comfort Zone: Lessons of Intercultural Service." *Clearing House,* 2009, *82,* 81–89.

Vande Berg, M., and Paige, R. M. "The Evolution of Intercultural Competence in U.S. Study Abroad." In D. K. Deardorff (ed.), *The SAGE Handbook of Intercultural Competence.* Thousand Oaks, Calif.: Sage, 2009.

Based at Duke University, DARLA K. DEARDORFF is a noted scholar, widely published author, and editor of The Sage Handbook of Intercultural Competence *(2009), instructor/trainer, and consultant worldwide on issues related to intercultural competence development and assessment.*

NEW DIRECTIONS FOR INSTITUTIONAL RESEARCH • DOI: 10.1002/ir

7

Civic engagement of college students is readily endorsed as an aspiration in higher education; however, defining and assessing civic learning outcomes is challenging. This chapter brings clarity to the knowledge, skills, and dispositions of civic-minded graduates and offers advice on program development and assessment strategies to reach civic outcomes.

Assessing Civic Knowledge and Engagement

Julie A. Hatcher

Preparing graduates to be active citizens is a core value of colleges and universities in the United States (Knefelkamp, 2008; Sullivan, 2000). Historically, higher education has had a commitment to developing the civic commitment of its graduates; yet the degree to which this commitment is endorsed and actualized varies with time and across institutions (Stanton and Wagner, 2006; Thelin, 2004). The past two decades have seen renewed emphasis on the public purposes of higher education (Ehrlich, 2000). The Carnegie Foundation for the Advancement of Teaching now has a voluntary classification for "community engagement," and this new designation reinforces and elevates the emphasis given to this aspect of campus mission (Sandmann, Thornton, and Jaeger, 2009). However, reports by the Association of American Colleges and Universities (AACU, 2009) indicate that even though academic leaders endorse civic preparation, they also report few curricular or program strategies to reach this goal on their campuses. There is a gap between the real and ideal in terms of the degree to which programs cultivate the civic identity and participation of undergraduates (Knefelkamp, 2008).

In *College Learning for the New Global Century* (National Leadership Council for Liberal Education and America's Promise, 2007), consensus among colleges and universities is reflected in four broad essential learning outcomes for the twenty-first-century world. These four domains are knowledge of human cultures and the physical and natural world, intellectual and practical skills, personal and social responsibility, and integrative and applied learning. These domains for general education are also

NEW DIRECTIONS FOR INSTITUTIONAL RESEARCH, no. 149, Spring 2011 © Wiley Periodicals, Inc.
Published online in Wiley Online Library (wileyonlinelibrary.com) • DOI: 10.1002/ir.382

consistent with goals identified by future employers seeking qualified graduates to enter the twenty-first-century workplace (Hammang, 2010; Spiezio, 2009). The topic of this chapter falls within the domain of personal and social responsibility. The chapter defines civic engagement, identifies the knowledge and skills associated within civic learning outcomes, provides the theoretical foundation for development of civic identity, offers examples of successful program strategies, and describes how student learning outcomes can be assessed in general education programs.

Definitional Issues

In summer 2009, a Symposium on Assessing Students' Civic Outcomes was hosted by our Center for Service and Learning on the campus of Indiana University-Purdue University Indianapolis (IUPUI). Cosponsored by the American Association of State Colleges and Universities (AASCU) and the National Service Learning Clearinghouse, this symposium invited researchers from a variety of disciplines to share and map efforts to assess college student civic engagement so participants could build on each other's work and advance research in the field (Keen, 2009). Participants noted the problem of many definitions of student civic engagement, with each definition leading to its own assessment instrument. Such definitional issues are often symptomatic of an emerging field and areas of study such as civic engagement (Hatcher, 2010).

As participants on the Civic Engagement Rubric development team for the AACU Valid Assessment of Learning in Undergraduate Education project (Rhodes, 2010), our team of eleven faculty and staff concurred that there were differences in definitions of civic engagement in the literature; some definitions emphasized action while others emphasized democratic processes (Saltmarsh, Hartley, and Clayton, 2009). We could all agree on what a civically engaged student "looked like," but it was much more challenging to come to agreement on a common definition. Our group concluded that the following definition was most appropriate to include in the Civic Engagement Rubric (AACU, 2009) to assess student learning in the domain of civic knowledge and engagement:

> Civic engagement is working to make a difference in the civic life of our communities and developing the combination of knowledge, skills, values, and motivation to make that difference. It means promoting the quality of life in a community, through both political and non-political processes [Ehrlich, 2000, p. vi].

Research under way, through the Center for Social Development at Washington University, on the International Volunteer Impacts Survey (Lough, McBride, and Sherradan, 2009) also uses this definition of civic engagement. Their research confirms that the construct is broad and comprises four independent, yet related, subconcepts: civic activism, community engagement, media attentiveness, and financial contributions. Additionally, the construct includes a range of behaviors, from volunteering to voting (Lough, McBride, and Sherradan, 2009).

Carol Musil (2009, p. 59) offers another definition, suggesting that "civic engagement is acting on a heightened sense of responsibility to one's communities that encompasses the notions of global citizenship and interdependence, participation in building civil society, and empowering individuals as agents of positive social change to promote social justice locally and globally."

Both of these definitions include active participation based on personal values and a sense of civic responsibility to improve society. The second definition is more expansive in its inclusion of global citizenship and social justice. Faculty must deliberate and come to a consensus on a definition of civic engagement that is most appropriate for program, campus, and institutional contexts, because the definition of civic engagement will ultimately frame and guide your assessment strategies.

Conceptual Frameworks and Theoretical Foundations

In developing the AACU Civic Engagement Rubric, our working group concluded that the "civic learning spiral" developed by the AACU (Leskes and Miller, 2006) was the strongest conceptual framework on which to build the rubric (Rhodes, 2010). The value of the civic learning spiral lies in its delineation of learning outcomes across six elements, or braids, that coexist simultaneously and are interconnected: self, communities and culture, knowledge, skills, values, and public action. These domains shape learning for both curricular and co-curricular experiences (Musil, 2009).

Colby and Damon (1992) sought to explain the "developmental process" that contributes to the origins of moral commitment. They identified six common characteristics of moral exemplars: learned optimism, sense of gratitude, personal integrity, strong social networks, faith, and moral reflection. They noted that a strong tie to others reinforced a strong sense of personal identity and personal goals; social networks bring a sense of clarity and commitment to the moral purposes of individuals. Thus interaction with others develops personal identity, and at the same time personal identity brings forth a stronger commitment to the public good. Indeed, interaction with peers has been found to be one of the essential components of sustaining and developing civic commitment during the college years (Strayhorn, 2008).

Civic Knowledge

The type of knowledge that is considered within the domain of "civic knowledge" is dependent, in part, on disciplinary perspectives. Political science may emphasize knowledge of political action, how a bill becomes a law, or the role of organizations to lobby and shape public policy. Philanthropic studies may emphasize knowledge of nonprofit organizations, social movements, or the role of voluntary action. Social work may emphasize the role of advocacy, collective action, or social justice. Just as the disciplines inform a variety of conceptual frameworks for the word *citizen* and delineation of civic skills (Battistoni, 2002), so too the disciplines inform the type of knowledge that comprises civic knowledge.

In addition to discipline-specific knowledge, there is a particular understanding about knowledge itself that constitutes the concept of civic knowledge. This frame of reference is evident in the civic learning spiral in that civic knowledge includes recognition that knowledge is dynamic, changing, and consistently reevaluated; understanding that knowledge is socially constructed and implicated with power; familiarity with key historical struggles, campaigns, and social movements to achieve the full promise of democracy; deep knowledge about the fundamental principles of and central arguments about democracy over time, as expressed in the United States and in other countries; and the ability to describe the main civic intellectual debates within one's major (Musil, 2009).

Another characteristic of civic knowledge is an understanding that "knowledge is actionable and that individuals coming together to co-create knowledge empowers them to make positive change in the world around them" (Longo and Shaffer, 2009, p. 169). This concept of democratic knowledge validates that knowledge is co-created in partnership with communities, students, and others (Saltmarsh, Hartley, and Clayton, 2009).

Civic Skills

In terms of civic skills, a variety of skills have been identified as supporting the capacity for civic engagement. Daloz, Keen, Keen, and Parks (1996) interviewed 145 adults to understand how active citizenship is developed. Several skills associated with active citizenship were identified, among them dialogue, interpersonal perspective taking, and critical systematic thought. Further research by Keen and Hall (2008) found that "dialogue across difference" was the most critical skill in the development of civic commitments among young adults who were participants in the Bonner Scholar Program during college. Civic discourse and dialogue were also common skills identified by many of the participants in the IUPUI Symposium on Assessing Civic Outcomes (Keen, 2010).

In a working paper published by CIRCLE, a set of civic skills were identified by Mary Kirlin (2003), based on a comprehensive review of the literature in political science, education, and psychology. Kirlin presented four major categories of civic skills: organization, communication, collective decision making, and critical thinking. Examples of civic skills are organizing and persuading others to take action, navigating the political system, consensus building toward the common good, listening to diverse perspectives, and forming positions on public issues. These civic skills are also consistent with the participatory skills identified by the National Assessment of Educational Progress: Civics Consensus Project (U.S. Department of Education, 1998).

Civic Identity

Literature and research to date confirm the importance of identity as either a contributing factor or a fundamental aspect of civic engagement (Colby and Damon, 1992; Daloz, Keen, Keen, and Parks, 1996). The term *civic identity* describes the aspect of identity that leads one to take public action (Colby and Sullivan, 2009; Knefelkamp, 2008; Youniss, McLellan, and Yates, 1997). Civic identity is when people see themselves as active participants in society with a strong commitment to work with others toward the public good.

This sense of civic identity, combined with cultivation of purpose and the ability to put knowledge to responsible and practical use (Colby and Sullivan, 2009), is critical to understanding why civic engagement occurs. Consistent with college student development theory, the formation of civic identity develops over time through engagement with others.

Civic identity is related to both intellectual and ethical development, includes critical thinking and empathy for others, and is a deliberately chosen and repeated aspect of self (Knefelkamp, 2008). Research indicates that participation in organized groups during adolescence is fundamental in formation of civic identity (Youniss, McLellan, and Yates, 1997). There is a growing body of evidence that participation and peer interaction during the college years contribute to formation of lifelong civic commitments (Strayhorn, 2008).

Practices That Lead to Civic Learning Outcomes

There are numerous examples of practices used inside the classroom and through co-curricular activities to foster development of civic knowledge, skill, identity, and behavior (Colby, Ehrlich, Beaumont, and Stephens, 2003; Colby, Ehrlich, Beaumont, and Corngold, 2007; Jacoby and Associates, 2009). Student leadership programs, political action activities, and classroom teaching strategies all contribute in important ways to development of civic identity during the college years. Three practices are highlighted here.

Service Learning. The curricular strategy most clearly aligned with civic learning outcomes is service learning (Dey and others, 2009). Although there are many forms of community involvement and civic engagement, service learning represents one of the best approaches for reaching the most central goals of teaching students civic knowledge, skills, and habits (Battistoni, 2000; Eyler and Giles, 1999; Moely and others, 2002). Service learning is defined as a "course-based, credit-bearing educational experience in which students (a) participate in an organized service activity that meets identified community needs and (b) reflect on the service activity in such a way as to gain further understanding of course content, a broader appreciation of the discipline, and an enhanced sense of personal values and civic responsibility" (Bringle and Hatcher, 1995, p. 112). In contrast to many other examples of applied learning and community-based instruction such as cooperative education, field studies, or internships, service learning has as an intentional educational goal: the civic education and growth of students. Designing structured reflection activities (Hatcher, Bringle, and Muthiah, 2004) to reach these civic goals is fundamental to the success of this pedagogy; service in and of itself may or may not lead to civic outcomes (Ash, Clayton, and Atkinson, 2005).

The Classroom as Democratic Environment. Another course-based strategy is to transform the classroom into a democratic environment that supports and cultivates civic learning outcomes. This strategy views the classroom as more than simply a learning environment; it "also functions as a social and a political system" (Spiezio, 2009, p. 90) that invites and challenges students to develop and practice civic skills. Students take personal responsibility for their own learning, influence governance of the class, participate in peer assessment, and function as co-educators with faculty. An empirical study of Participating in Democracy Project, a model that was field-tested at eight college and universities through funding by the Teagle Foundation and Atlantic Philanthropic, demonstrated "measurable and significant differences between students enrolled in Democratic Academy classrooms and the general student population in terms of student learning outcomes relevant to the promotion of social capital" (Speizio, 2009, p. 86). Teaching resources developed from the project are readily available (Meade and Weaver, 2004).

Service-Based Scholarship Programs. The third practice to highlight is service-based scholarship programs. The Bonner Foundation's Bonner Scholars Program is a co-curricular program that supports four-year community service scholarships for students attending twenty-seven colleges and universities. A number of program evaluations demonstrate that there are multiple benefits for students, faculty, and community partners (Keen and Hall, 2008). Influenced by a pivotal finding in earlier research (Daloz, Keen, Keen, and Parks, 1996), civic discourse is repeatedly woven into this program to foster civic engagement in adulthood. The Bonner Scholar Program is a cohort-based model that includes ongoing opportunities for interaction with others and dialogue across difference, and this is the component of the program that students report to be most valuable (Keen and Hall, 2008). On our own campus, we have designed the Sam H. Jones Community Service Scholarship Program to support the involvement of students in educationally meaningful service experiences (Hatcher, Bringle, Brown, and Fleischhacker, 2006). Through seven types of service-based scholarships, more than 175 students annually participate in community service, lead peers in service activities, assist faculty with implementing service learning classes, and participate in structured reflection activities. Service scholars gain leadership skills and have opportunities to be change agents on campus and in the community. Program evaluation indicates that service scholars report greater gains in civic outcomes than their peers who are not involved in cohort-based service programs.

Assessment Measures

There are many examples of ways to assess civic learning outcomes, whether through course-level or campus-level assessment strategies (Keen, 2009; see also the Bonner Foundation Network Wiki, the IUPUI Center for Service and Learning website, and the National Service Learning Clearinghouse Research Hub websites for sample measures). In addition, there are some excellent examples of longitudinal research under way at the institutional level to assess the long-term impact of civic engagement activities. Researchers at Tufts University and the University of Notre Dame have strong longitudinal research designs and findings that will shed light on which activities during the college years are of particular importance in terms of developing a civic identity.

However, assessment strategies for civic engagement are yet to fully be integrated into most campus cultures. Bringle and Hatcher (2009) examined dossiers from the first cohort of campuses that successfully applied for the Carnegie Classification for Community Engagement and concluded that the evidence presented to evaluate the extent to which service learning courses and other community-based courses met intended learning outcomes mirrors general assessment practice in higher education. Of particular concern was the finding that assessment in this first cohort was heavily dependent on self-report instruments. Some aggregation of data across the curriculum was reported, but it was quite limited and with little coordination to other forms of institutional research and institutional evaluation. The *College Student Report*, developed as part of the National Survey of Student Engagement (NSSE), was one example cited that permits comparison with peer institutions. Another example was the *College Senior Survey (CSS)* developed by the Higher Education Research Institute at the University of California, Los Angeles. Both questionnaires are limited in that they capture only student self-reports of the level of involvement in a limited range of civic activities.

The AACU Civic Engagement Rubric holds promise for assessing authentic student learning products such as e-portfolios. The rubric was designed by a team representing various disciplinary perspectives, went through three rounds of drafting, was field tested by a number of faculty, and was modified on the basis of feedback (Rhodes, 2010). The rubric contains six categories: diversity of communities and cultures, analysis of knowledge, civic identity and commitment, civic communication, civic action and reflection, and civic contexts and structures. Four levels are described to capture growth, from the benchmark level to the capstone level, for each category. This rubric is a tool that can be adapted and modified to align more closely with campus climate, curricular learning goals, or course-based outcomes. Along with twelve other rubrics to assess general education outcomes, it is available on the AACU website (www.aacu.org/value/rubrics/).

The AASCU has also focused on assessment of civic learning outcomes through both the American Democracy Project (Mehaffey, 2009) and the Degrees of Preparation survey funded by the Fund for the Improvement of Postsecondary Education (Hammang, 2010). The survey is designed to measure gains from the entering year to graduation, with questions "capable of measuring students' increasing preparation for participation in civic engagement, preparation for success in the workplace, and the acquisition of global skills" (Hammang, 2010, p. 8). The survey also includes an open-ended narrative prompt for students to share their personal experiences related to work and community engagement. Researchers found that students were quite willing to write about their personal experiences, and the narratives provide valuable stories that institutional leadership can use to illustrate and underscore the value of student preparation during the college years. This survey is still in the development phase and holds strong promise as a tool for institutional assessment of civic preparation during the college years.

Over the past five years, our Center for Service and Learning at IUPUI has identified the concept "civic-minded graduate" (CMG) as the "north star" for program development, assessment, and research. This work is based on an extensive literature review and consensus among program staff to identify a common set of learning outcomes for our students. We have defined a civic-minded graduate as one who is formally educated and has the capacity and orientation to work with others democratically to improve the community. Civic-mindedness is a person's inclination or disposition to be knowledgeable of and involved in the community, and to commit to act on a sense of responsibility as a member of that community (Bringle and Steinberg, 2010). As shown in Figure 7.1, the concept of CMG represents the intersection of three student attributes: self-identity, academic knowledge and skills, and civic attitudes and participation.

The thirty-item CMG scale addresses ten domains, among them knowledge of volunteer opportunities and contemporary social issues, skills in listening, diversity, consensus building, and the disposition to value community engagement in their lives and through their future career (Bringle and Steinberg, 2010). We have conducted two studies

Figure 7.1.

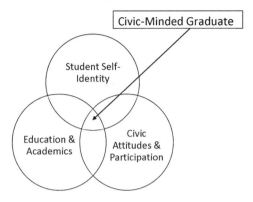

using the CMG scale, and the measure has good reliability. More important, the CMG Narrative Prompt and the accompanying CMG Rubric have been designed as tools to gather and assess authentic student work, evaluate civic learning outcomes, and validate the CMG scale. Authentic student work may be a student narrative, a student project, or a student e-portfolio. Both of these assessment tools can be found at http://csl.iupui.edu/assessment/classroomtools.cfm.

Consistent with other strategies for assessing civic outcomes (Hammang, 2010), we found that students were quite willing to write answers in response to the CMG Narrative Prompt, either as a course-based assignment or as an open-ended question at the end of the online survey format. The CMG Narrative Prompt is phrased as shown here, with key words italicized to focus attention to each component of the prompt:

> I have a responsibility and a commitment to use the knowledge and skills I have gained as a college student to collaborate with others, *who may be different from me,* to help address issues in society.
>
> Please indicate the extent to which you agree or disagree with this statement by circling the appropriate number.
>
> Strongly   Strongly
> Disagree   Agree
> 1   2   3   4   5   6
>
> Considering your education and experiences as a college student, explain the ways in which you agree or disagree with this statement and provide personal examples when relevant.

Short and long answers on the CMG Narrative Prompt can be evaluated using the CMG Rubric, and both types have been found to positively correlate with results on the CMG survey. Departments have adapted the CMG Survey, Narrative, and Rubric to assess discipline-specific outcomes.

Conclusion

Civic engagement is a complex term, and there are a variety of ways to involve college students in meaningful action that improves communities. Forms of civic engagement depend, in part, on campus mission and climate, administrative support, faculty disciplinary perspectives, student leadership, political climate, and community context. Much like the civic learning spiral (Musil, 2009), weaving together all of these braids creates a civic engagement spiral for each campus to enact and assess its civic engagement goals.

Institutional assessment plays an important role in improving practice in higher education. Gathering systematic data permits insight into campus culture, faculty work, and student learning. As more campuses devote resources to support development of service learning classes and civic engagement programs, it is important that assessment strategies produce information on trends, program outcomes, and effective curricular strategies. Higher education has the capacity to influence change in student learning, and also in communities and society through the active engagement of students, faculty, and graduates.

Through systematic assessment, we can gain understanding and take new and refined action to support change. John Dewey (1927) described this knowledge as social intelligence; such knowledge can lead to change, can improve society, and is vital to preserving and advancing democracy. As educators and reflective practitioners in higher education, we will do well to advance the assessment of civic learning outcomes.

References

American Association of Colleges and Universities (AACU). "VALUE Rubrics, VALUE: Valid Assessment of Learning in Undergraduate Education." 2009. Retrieved July 14, 2010, from http://www.aacu.org/value/metarubrics.cfm.

Ash, S., Clayton, P., and Atkinson, M. "Integrating Reflection and Assessment to Capture and Improve Student Learning." *Michigan Journal of Community Service-Learning*, 2005, *11*(2), 49–60.

Battistoni, R. "Service Learning and Civic Education." In S. Mann and J. Patrick (eds.), *Education for Civic Engagement in Democracy: Service Learning and Other Promising Practices.* Educational Research Information Center, Indiana University, 2000.

Battistoni, R. *Civic Engagement Across the Curriculum: A Resource Book for Service-Learning Faculty in All Disciplines.* Providence, R.I.: Campus Compact, 2002.

Bringle, R., and Hatcher, J. "A Service-Learning Curriculum for Faculty." *Michigan Journal of Community Service Learning*, 1995, 2, 112–122.

Bringle, R., and Hatcher, J. "Innovative Practices in Service Learning and Curricular Engagement." In *Institutionalizing Community Engagement in Higher Education: The First Wave of Carnegie Classified Institutions.* (Special Issue.) New Directions for Higher Education, no. 147, 2009, 37–46.

Bringle, R., and Steinberg, K. "Educating for Informed Community Involvement." *American Journal of Community Psychology*, 2010, *46*, 428–441..

Colby, A., and Damon, W. *Some Do Care: Contemporary Lives of Moral Commitment.* New York: Free Press, 1992.

Colby, A., Ehrlich, T., Beaumont, E., and Corngold, J. *Educating for Democracy: Preparing Undergraduates for Responsible Political Engagement.* San Francisco: Jossey-Bass, 2007.

Colby, A., Ehrlich, T., Beaumont, E., and Stephens, J. *Educating Citizens: Preparing America's Undergraduates for Lives of Moral and Civic Responsibility.* San Francisco: Jossey-Bass, 2003.

Colby, A., and Sullivan, W. "Strengthening the Foundations of Student's Excellence, Integrity, and Social Contribution." *Liberal Education,* 2009, *95*(1), 22–29.

Daloz, L., Keen, C., Keen, J., and Parks, S. *Common Fire: Lives of Commitment in a Complex World.* Boston: Beacon Press, 1996.

Dewey, J. *The Public and Its Problems.* Athens: Ohio University Press, 1927.

Dey, E., Barnhardt, C., Antonaros, M., Ott, M., and Holsapple, M. *Civic Responsibility: What Is the Campus Climate for Learning?* Washington, D.C.: Association of American Colleges and Universities, 2009.

Ehrlich, T. *Civic Responsibility and Higher Education.* Phoenix, Ariz.: Oryx, 2000.

Eyler, J., and Giles, D. *Where's the Learning in Service-Learning?* San Francisco: Jossey-Bass, 1999.

Hammang, J. "Beginning to Measure Learning Outcomes Affecting the Public Good." In Association of American Colleges and Universities (ed.), *Rising to the Challenge: Meaningful Assessment of Student Learning Outcomes.* Washington, DC: American Association of State Colleges and Universities, Association for Public and Land-Grant Universities, 2010.

Hatcher, J. "Defining the Catchphrase: Understanding the Civic Engagement of College Students." *Michigan Journal of Community Service Learning,* 2010, *16*(2), 95–100.

Hatcher, J., Bringle, R., Brown, L., and Fleischhacker, D. "Supporting Student Involvement Through Service-Based Scholarships." In E. Zlotkowski, N. Longo, and J. Williams (eds.), *Students as Colleagues: Expanding the Circle of Service-Learning Leadership.* Providence, R.I.: Campus Compact, 2006.

Hatcher, J., Bringle, R., and Muthiah, R. "Designing Effective Reflection: What Matters to Service-Learning?" *Michigan Journal of Community Service-Learning,* 2004, *11*(1), 38–46.

Jacoby, B., and Associates. *Civic Engagement in Higher Education: Concepts and Practices.* San Francisco: Jossey-Bass, 2009.

Keen, C. "New Efforts to Assess Civic Outcomes." *Journal of College and Character,* 2009, *10*(7), 1–6.

Keen, C. "Measuring Dialogue Across Difference as a Civic Skill." *Journal of College and Character,* 2010, *11*(1), 1–8.

Keen, C., and Hall, K. "Post-Graduation Service and Civic Outcomes for High Financial Need Students of a Multi-Campus, Co-Curricular Service-Learning College Program." *Journal of College and Character,* 2008, *10*(2), 1–15.

Kirlin, M. *The Role of Civic Skills in Fostering Civic Engagement.* CIRCLE Working Paper 6. Center for Information and Research on Civic Learning and Engagement, University of Maryland, 2003.

Knefelkamp, L. "Civic Identity: Locating Self in Community." *Diversity and Democracy: Civic Learning for Shared Futures,* 2008, *11*(2), 1–3.

Leskes, A., and Miller, R. *Purposeful Pathways: Helping Student Achieve Key Learning Outcomes.* Washington, D.C.: Association of American Colleges and Universities, 2006.

Longo, N., and Shaffer, P. "Leadership Education and the Revitalization of Public Life." In B. Jacoby (ed.), *Civic Engagement in Higher Education: Concepts and Practices.* San Francisco: Jossey-Bass, 2009.

Lough, B., McBride, A., and Sherradan, M. "Measuring Volunteer Outcomes: Development of the International Volunteer Impacts Survey." 2009. Retrieved July 14, 2010, from http://csd.wustl.edu/ Publications/Documents/WP09-31.pdf.

Meade, E., and Weaver, S. *Toolkit for Teaching in a Democratic Academy.* Allentown, Pa.: Cedar Crest College, 2004.

Mehaffy, G. *Report on the Symposium on Assessing Students' Civic Outcomes.* Unpublished. American Association of State Colleges and Universities, 2009.

Moely, B., Mercer, S., Ilustre, V., Miron, D., and McFarland, M. "Psychometric Properties and Correlates of the Civic Attitudes and Skills Questionnaire (CASQ): A Measure of Students' Attitudes Related to Service-Learning." *Michigan Journal of Community Service-Learning,* 2002, 8(2), 15–26.

Musil, C. "Educating Students for Personal and Social Responsibility: The Civic Learning Spiral." In B. Jacoby (ed.), *Civic Engagement in Higher Education: Concepts and Practices.* San Francisco: Jossey-Bass, 2009.

National Leadership Council for Liberal Education and America's Promise. *College Learning for the New Global Century.* Washington, D.C.: Association of American Colleges and Universities, 2007.

Rhodes, T. (ed.). *Assessing Outcomes and Improving Achievement: Tips and Tools for Using Rubrics.* Washington, D.C.: Association of American Colleges and Universities, 2010.

Saltmarsh, J., Hartley, M., and Clayton, P. *Democratic Engagement White Paper.* Boston: New England Resource Center for Higher Education, 2009.

Sandmann, L., Thornton, C., and Jaeger, A. (eds.). *Institutionalizing Community Engagement in Higher Education: The First Wave of Carnegie Classified Institutions.* (Special Issue.) New Directions for Higher Education, no. 147. San Francisco: Jossey-Bass, 2009.

Spiezio, K. "Engaging General Education." In B. Jacoby and Associates (eds.), *Civic Engagement in Higher Education: Concepts and Practices.* San Francisco: Jossey Bass, 2009.

Stanton, T., and Wagner, J. *Education for Democratic Citizenship: Renewing the Civic Mission of Graduate and Professional Education at Research Universities.* Position paper prepared for Stanford Symposium on Civic Engagement and Graduate Education at Research Universities, Stanford University, Palo Alto, Calif., Apr. 24, 2006.

Strayhorn, T. "How College Students' Engagement Affects Personal and Social Learning Outcomes." *Journal of College and Character,* 2008, 10(2), 1–16.

Sullivan, W. "Institutional Identity and Social Responsibility in Higher Education." In T. Ehrlich (ed.), *Civic Responsibility and Higher Education.* Phoenix, Ariz.: Oryx Press, 2000.

Thelin, J. *A History of American Higher Education.* Baltimore: John Hopkins University Press, 2004.

U.S. Department of Education. "Civic Education Survey." 1998. Retrieved July 14, 2010, from http://nces.ed.gov/surveys/cived/.

Youniss, J., McLellan, J., and Yates, M. "What We Know About Engendering Civic Identity." *American Behavioral Scientist,* 1997, 40(5), 620–631.

JULIE A. HATCHER *is associate professor of philanthropic studies, through the Center on Philanthropy in the School of Liberal Arts, and a senior scholar with the Center for Service and Learning at Indiana University-Purdue University Indianapolis.*

NEW DIRECTIONS FOR INSTITUTIONAL RESEARCH • DOI: 10.1002/ir

We examine the concept of integrative and applied learning from various perspectives, emphasize transfer of that learning to unfamiliar and unimagined settings, and describe crucial metacognitive strategies, including learned abilities used as frameworks for performance, reflection, and self-assessment that foster learning that lasts. We follow with examples of Alverno approaches for assessing these complex capacities across a curriculum.

How We Know It When We See It: Conceptualizing and Assessing Integrative and Applied Learning-In-Use

Marcia Mentkowski, Stephen Sharkey

Perhaps you have had the experience of talking to faculty about the ups and downs of their students' achievement, and hearing them describe what they consider good work. Almost inevitably, such conversation will include phrases like "She got it all together," "He used material from prior courses to frame his research," "She applied what she learned earlier this term to analyze a new problem or situation," "His portfolio showed he could reflect on his evolution as a learner over time," or "She has a real sense of herself as a liberally educated person who serves and leads." Our experience tells us that faculty from quite different fields often use very similar language to describe this "getting it all together and using it" and have long debated factors in their teaching or curricula that can make more of "it" happen for more students.

The authors acknowledge the AACU Valid Assessment of Learning in Undergraduate Education (VALUE) Rubric Development Team for Integrative and Applied Learning: Elizabeth J. Ciner, Carleton College; Ariane Hoy, Bonner Foundation; Kate Lang, University of Wisconsin–Eau Claire; Adam Lutzker, University of Michigan–Flint; Jean Mach, College of San Mateo; Marcia Mentkowski, Alverno College; Francine G. Navakas, North Central College; Judy Patton, Portland State University; Candyce Reynolds, Portland State University; William Rickards, Alverno College; and Judith Stanley, Alverno College. Marcia Mentkowski and Ariane Hoy served on the advisory board for the VALUE project.

On the other hand, we have also observed faculty reluctant to pursue this discussion too far, especially if it is initiated by an assessment committee that seems to be talking about measuring such a complex act of learning with some battery of tests. Questions get raised: What is integration? Is application a lower- or higher-order skill? How might integrative and applied learning as a college outcome transfer to settings that students have not yet experienced or even imagined (Mentkowski, 2009)? Some faculty and administrators might even go so far as to say that this thing called integrative and applied learning cannot really be measured, in an authentic sense, because it is too ephemeral. Some argue that such judgments are better left to the teachers and advisors closest to the students and their work.

How can a campus agree on such matters? What might it mean to work across disciplines at your campus to reevaluate and redefine integrative and applied learning as postcollege environments change? As Alverno educators and scholars, our work has taken us into the heart of this debate, and so we and our colleagues have come to some useful ideas and strategies: (1) how to define integrative and applied learning in ways that assist a cross-disciplinary faculty to better evaluate students across courses and over time; and (2) how to build an assessment system that can capture and use information from student electronic portfolios to meaningfully evaluate programs for contributions to this complex yet essential student learning outcome.

In this chapter, we share some key results from discussions, research, reflective practices, and others' perspectives on assisting students to engage and demonstrate integrative and applied learning. First, we traverse the definitional territory of this complex construct, referring to the national literature and discussion as well as our own studies to give shape to the ideas. Second, we lay out features of the type of campus assessment system and culture necessary to meaningfully capture and use information about integration and application for improving teaching for student learning. Third, we offer three examples of Alverno faculty-designed, campuswide, and required assessment instruments currently in use. Each assessment yields faculty judgments of achievement at the level of the individual student, who also uses the evaluative information for formative and summative purposes. The assessment also generates judgments of program effectiveness for faculty members who use synthesized assessment data diagnostically for curriculum improvement and for discussions with colleagues from various consortia of institutions.

Defining the Territory: A Key National Project

In 2004, Huber and Hutchings set the stage for collaboration on integrative learning and found support from the American Association of Colleges and Universities (AACU), which made grants to various campuses, such as Portland State University and Carleton College, to encourage faculty to develop integrative learning projects such as portfolios and capstone seminars (Bierman and others, 2005).

Another major effort by AACU and the federal Department of Education was the VALUE Project: Valid Assessment of Learning in Undergraduate Education (AACU, 2009b). From the beginning, AACU leaders such as President Carol Geary Schneider emphasized including both integrative and applied learning. "Integrative and applied learning . . . is a truly twenty-first century liberal art," she wrote. "Students must now know how to apply knowledge and to use it in new contexts" (2008, p. 3). Schneider's observation became a challenge for the multicampus team, which included Alverno's faculty and educational researchers, who worked to develop the integrative and applied learning rubric.

This multicampus team agreed on a basic definition: "Integrative and applied learning is an understanding and a disposition that a student builds across the curriculum and co-curriculum, from making simple connections among ideas and experiences to synthesizing and transferring learning to new, complex situations within and beyond the campus" (AACU, 2009a; Rhodes, 2010). Elaborating on this, we can say that a definition of integrative and applied learning capable of generating valid and usable criteria for evaluating student work would need to incorporate several dimensions of relationship building all at once: relationships among past, present, and future learning; relationships between areas of study; and relationships between prior situations where learning was used and new situations where it could be used.

Thus the VALUE rubric evolved with five dimensions: connections to experience, connections to disciplines, transfer, integrated communication, and reflection and self-assessment (see AACU, 2009a). At the end of their set of meetings, rubric team members acknowledged that they had just begun to elaborate criteria and student performance descriptors for the five dimensions. Yet their exploration and analyses of concrete examples of assessment practices on campuses around the country had built a solid base for further work.

Educational Theory, Research, and Practice at Alverno

Much of the AACU rubric team's work on integrative and applied learning dovetailed with our own at Alverno. For example, we strongly agree with our AACU colleagues and the broader educational research community that relationship building between integrative and applied learning is essential for individuals developing an emergent sense of personal mastery or expertise (Feltovich, Prietula, and Ericsson, 2006). For another, we know that college learning transfers to workplace learning provided students have developed a web of relationships between thinking and action (Eraut, 1994; Rogers and Mentkowski, 2004; Schön, 1987).

New Directions for Institutional Research • DOI: 10.1002/ir

Yet educators may ask, How might such statements translate into concrete pedagogy and assessment? To effectively teach and assess for integrative and applied learning, we rely on multiple sources of ideas, evidence, and contexts of practice. These include reviews of theory and research literature and practices of other institutions in our collaborating consortia. We fine-tune practices through our own educational theory and research, curriculum development processes, faculty scholarship of teaching, continuous revision of pedagogical practices based on student performances, and faculty discussion with colleagues in various institutional consortia (Mentkowski and Associates, 2000; Student Learning Initiative, 2002).

In the next section, we consider two critical points for new faculty taking up the teaching and assessment of integrative and applied learning. First, knowing and doing are intimately connected; second, integration and application come together in a performance.

Knowing and Doing Are Intimately Connected. Alverno's assessment work emphasizes this point with particular energy, because a central pedagogical principle we adhere to is that learning involves doing something with what one knows. Assessments emphasize performance, making visible how students use what they have studied through such tools as portfolios, simulations, projects, and written or oral presentations. In addition, we know that this cycle of knowing and doing can start very early in college. It can and should be encouraged through careful development of beginning-level assessments that elicit evidence of this kind of cycling. Our earliest studies of student development quite clearly indicated that the traditional vision of students first learning to do practical things without much complex thought, and then learning to theorize and conceptualize when they are more sophisticated, was misleading; both aspects of learning evolve together in a cyclical fashion (Mentkowski and Doherty, 1984). Using data based on Kolb's measure of learning styles (1976), we found it is empirically true that beginning college students often prefer learning through concrete experience, but they also begin a measurable shift toward preferring abstract conceptualization.

Integration and Application Come Together in a Performance. The term *performance assessment* is now quite common in the assessment literature. Performance assessment refers to tools and strategies that can detect and amplify students' learning-in-use, and yield information about how well students are integrating theory and practice that can help educators improve their curricula.

As early advocates of the concept, Alverno educators have emphasized how authentic assessments elicit opportunities for effective, thoughtful action by students in a particular context or situation. This is what our teaching colleagues usually mean by "We know integration and application when we see it." Where they see it is in an authentic performance assessment, where students' ideas, information, and effective use in addressing an issue or situation show up at the same time. Examples of such authentic performance assessments are myriad, but three areas common to Alverno and many other campuses are internships, capstones, and student research projects, where real problems and professional-level expectations for results are part of the assessment scenario. Yet we know effective assessment programs also seek ways to probe this growth in earlier phases of college. Furthermore, if authentic performances are synthesized and collectively analyzed, they generate needed information about how to improve a program (Alverno College Faculty, 1979/1994; Loacker and Mentkowski, 1993; Loacker and Rogers, 2005; Mentkowski and Loacker, 1985).

To heed Schneider's call to envision integrative and applied learning as a twenty-first-century liberal art, we now turn to three additional considerations. First, performance is a domain of growth in the person that develops in an integrated liberal arts and professions education. Second, learning to perform implies learning to transfer across a course of study and over time. Third, reflection and self-assessment are essential components of an assessment process that fosters integrative and applied learning (Mentkowski and Associates, 2000).

Performance Develops in an Integrated Liberal Arts and Professions Education. Research performed by Alverno's faculty showed that the convergence between liberal arts education and professions education was best carried out by designing general education and the majors as a connected set of common learning outcomes and requiring these outcomes for graduation. These outcomes are taught and assessed within and across courses from freshman through senior year. Faculty have determined and constantly revised a set of eight developmentally defined abilities that they use to design particular assessments, courses, and programs that unify the curriculum conceptually and experientially for students, no matter what their path of study.

Abilities are multidimensional learning outcomes that ultimately involve student integration of knowledge and understanding, behaviors and skills, attitudes and self-perceptions, motivations and dispositions, and habits of mind and values (Anastasi, 1980; Sternberg, 1998). Thus educators defined abilities as learned across a curriculum, integrated in the person, teachable, assessable, and transferable across settings. Students learned to perform abilities when they were assessed in multiple contexts in general education, the disciplines, and professions, rather than in separate courses. Educators determined pedagogical, sequential, or developmental levels to support teaching, and abilities have been constantly redefined through performance descriptors or criteria for student assessment. Consequently, Alverno faculty have expected abilities to be inferred from observable student performance.

Over time, as students encounter these abilities and see how their general definitions are adapted to the contexts of particular disciplines and course material, the abilities become a set of metacognitive strategies, a mental architecture students explicitly employ to build various relationships between the parts of their educational experience. Our research showed learners became adept at using their learned abilities—integrated with disciplinary frameworks—as metacognitive strategies for connecting their reasoning with their performance in unfamiliar settings (see Mentkowski and Associates, 2000; Rogers, Mentkowski, and Reisetter Hart, 2006). In more beginning performances, instructors observed students learning every facet of what a good performance was and putting some of them together. They found, too, that it was good explicit feedback about this process of integrating and applying other dimensions of learned abilities, such as synthesizing emotion with cognition or their own perceptions of a situation with those of others, that enabled students to better move along this novice-to-expert continuum and increasingly internalize this movement as part of their personal identity as performers and professionals.

Learning to Perform Involves Learning to Transfer. Faculty members have long intuited that students who can integrate and apply learning well are also good at transferring their learning from one context or situation to another. They can adapt what they know to new demands.

More precisely, following Holyoak (1991) we can say that a strong transferer will adapt what he or she knows and has applied before to construct a new performance informed by prior experience, with enough flexibility to manage the ambiguities and approximations this process of refining and judgment entails. Holyoak calls this adaptive expertise, as opposed to routine expertise in which a set of templates are applied over and over again. For learning to last across time and situations—what most educators are truly seeking, after all—students must develop this sort of adaptive flexibility, which rests on the ability to transfer, which in turn is built with opportunities for integration and application (Bransford, Brown, and Cocking, 2000; Lobato, 2003; Rogers and Mentkowski, 2004).

Reflection and Self-Assessment. As noted, self-reflection is a domain of growth in the person. In our research, we found that students and alumnae who successfully engaged in self-reflection that was perceptive, insightful, and adaptive confirmed that faculty members had taught them the *self-assessment process*: to observe their performance, interpret and analyze it, provide their own feedback and seek that of others, and judge its effectiveness in relation to criteria that afford a picture of their developing abilities. Students also became able to plan for further learning, and by graduation, to generate their own criteria.

From studies of the in-depth perspectives of Alverno students and alumnae on how they learned, faculty had learned to do more than invite students to do self-assessment. They taught them how and created structured opportunities for them to reflect (Alverno College Faculty, 2000; Mentkowski and Associates, 2000). Alverno faculty routinely include explicit self-assessment components in all their performance assessments, and they evaluate both the student work itself and often the quality of the self-assessment.

Alverno research further shows that self-assessment of performance in various roles is another transformative learning cycle that boosts students' capacity to integrate and apply. Alumnae also showed that they carry self-assessment forward with them into their personal and professional lives, as they seek to define what they ought to be doing in a situation or to improve their performance (see Mentkowski and Associates, 2000).

Campus Culture and the Assessment of Integrative and Applied Learning

We believe that to assess complex, multidimensional learning outcomes at the level of the individual student and program, a particular vision of educational and institutional research needs to pervade a campus. In many places, faculty members already enjoy a certain natural, informal sharing of ideas and experiences about student learning; in this sharing they can end up honing their sense of what students' integration and application looks like, and what likely helps them improve their adapting and transferring of developing abilities to unfamiliar settings.

Distinguishing Measurement and Judgment. Yet some may also be leery about talk of measurement, especially if those doing the measuring are distant researchers who present findings without feedback. Sometimes even faculty colleagues serving on an assessment committee can be challenged on multiple fronts, particularly if a committee fails to consider interdisciplinary meanings for assessment or how differently performance appears across the disciplines and professions. We think such concerns for measurement are intimately tied up with how the measuring is organized to occur on a campus: who does what, where, and when, with what sort of information, and with what actual results. We propose a particular understanding of program and institutional assessment to counter this. Assessing students' integrative and applied learning requires a set of processes that bring parties together more helpfully and collaboratively than may typically occur. This process starts from the premise that we need less to psychometrically *measure* integration and application than to *judge* it through expertly using rubrics and other forms of publicly shared criteria, with a special concern for observing how well students can transfer developing abilities to new situations. Consequently, the process also involves substantial work by faculty to learn how to assess in this way. This kind of approach has been successfully implemented on our own campus, and it has also influenced institutional assessment plan development on other campuses (Crain and Rogers, 2010; Mentkowski, 2006; Rogers, 1994).

Judging Dimensions and Levels with Criteria or Performance Descriptors. Here is the heart of the matter as we see it. To integrate and apply learning and transfer it to novel settings is a complex, multifaceted outcome of student development in a curriculum. For example, integrated communication is an outcome that many faculty members are used to teaching across disciplines. Sequential or developmental levels with specified criteria get at how faculty might teach integrated communication in a discipline and their experience of how students learn it. The VALUE rubric includes this dimension and is one current example of how to portray this complexity so as to help shape program evaluations. Yet whatever the strengths and weaknesses of this particular model, we are quite convinced that any effort to define the dynamic complexity of integrative and applied learning and how it connects to experience, disciplines, transfer, integrated communication, and reflection and self-assessment (the five dimensions of the rubric from AACU, 2009a) will acquire the sort of multidimensionality and developmental levels this rubric displays.

Using Multiple Strategies. Thus we share the strong doubts so many faculty and assessment specialists express over whether one clever instrument or procedure could do the job. Psychometric instruments can be helpful, and there are some out there to employ, but they all have important limits, as do performance assessments. Any data source should be used only as part of an array of information sources assembled for a more holistic analysis of student learning patterns in relationship to a curriculum. No one measure, no one data collection and evaluation system, can by itself discern the strength of students' integration and application in a sample performance. Effective use of multiple sources of data requires an intentional collaboration among the faculty and academic professionals who have generated them and whose future work is likely to be shaped by the findings. Their shared intention should be to align the college curriculum and co-curriculum with the goal of graduating learners who can integrate and apply, adapt and transfer what they have learned to settings these learners have not yet fully experienced or even imagined.

Evolving a Dynamic System. Given this, we affirm that to fully capture and aggregate as much as possible of the richness of such learning in a way educators can use, the assessment process and system must also be dynamic and complex. In effect, the assessment approach must mirror or match, draw on, and connect the aspects of the college experience the students themselves are going through. Observing integrative and applied learning and inferring capacities from performance demand an integrative assessment approach that elicits applied learning outcomes. Faculty and students as peer assessors need ways to observe, analyze and interpret, judge, and prepare feedback for a collection of a student's work—to get at how the student uses his or her integrative and applied learning.

Creating Social Arrangements. To truly assess integrative and applied learning, adapting and transferring, and observing learners using reflection and self-assessment of their performance on the spot, means to engage educators' interest in analyzing a range of samples of student work of various types and from various settings. It also means putting in place a *particular kind of social organization of assessment work* on a campus: one that rewards this engagement, facilitates the bringing together of evidence about student growth from venues on and off campus, and then uses that information in a series of faculty processes to better the curriculum. On the basis of our own systematic analyses of assessment work here at Alverno and elsewhere (Darling-Hammond, 2010; Diez, Athanasiou, and Pointer Mace, 2010; Loacker and Riordan, 2009; Riordan and Sharkey, 2010), we can be quite specific about effective assessment practices for highly complex outcomes such as integrative and applied learning, which at first may seem daunting to address, as in the chapter on assessing spirituality, "Assessing Ineffable Outcomes," by Chickering and Mentkowski (2006).

Developing a Community of Learning and Judgment. The same general principles described by Chickering and Mentkowski (2006) to explore the assessment of spirituality apply here. More specifically, assessment of integrative and applied learning requires creation of a *community of learning and judgment on campus.* By this we mean a set of norms, values, and organizational practices—a culture—that shape faculty time and energy around studying what integration and application might mean in principle; how they might tend to appear in actual student work; how to best design assignments and other tools to better reveal the developing ability to integrate and apply; how to judge the quality of students' integration and application coherently and fairly; and how to analyze the relationships between actual student performance on this developing ability, quality, or capacity and the features of the curriculum and co-curriculum students work through until graduation, and even beyond, if feasible.

Faculty and academic professionals see this sort of professional work as critical and meaningful, especially when criteria for tenure, promotion, and advancement express the value of doing the scholarship of teaching and learning that building and sustaining the community of learning and judgment requires. Gradually, Alverno's criteria for faculty advancement evolved, so that now they shape the growth of individual faculty in the direction of acquiring assessment expertise.

Building a Faculty Development Program. This expertise also needs to be shaped at the collective level by the approach taken to general faculty development, and there are multiple examples of success in this vein. Many faculty groups across the country have shown that faculty are capable of acting in consort on important issues that affect their students' learning (for example, at Wagner College; Guarasci and Lieberman, 2009). We agree with Levi and Stevens (2010) that when a faculty achieves some basic consensus about student educational outcomes, familiar stereotypes about faculty individualism-to-a-fault do not hold up. Time after time in working on campuses, we observe faculty coming to exciting consensus—not necessarily agreement—about what it means to be an educated person in remarkably short order, and they also are entirely able to articulate criteria for judgment that represent levels of achievement in samples of student work. This is also the case with more complex and seemingly ephemeral student learning outcomes such as integrative and applied capacities.

Assessing Integrative and Applied Learning at Alverno: Combined Program and Student Assessment

Alverno has been ceaselessly committed to connecting assessment of the institution and programs more directly to the process of student learning, so that assessment techniques at all levels become more of a total piece. This means creating the sort of campus culture described earlier, but also framing the design of assessment so as to rely heavily on direct student performances that can be aggregated and analyzed in various ways, whose information is primarily used to improve the quality of both individual student performance and programs as a whole. This general system has been described in a number of publications (see Alverno College Faculty, 1979/1994, 2000; Loacker and Mentkowski, 1993).

At the present time, dimensions of integrative and applied learning are tapped in three collegewide, criterion-based assessments that all students must complete successfully for graduation. They count because, in order to graduate, students must complete courses required for general education and their majors and support areas where they also demonstrate various levels of their developing abilities. Suffice it to say that the college also tracks student performance in required collegewide assessments administered outside of any one course by the Assessment Center. These are designed to assess integrative and applied learning, and transfer across courses and over time. Faculty from across the disciplines and professions are trained to assess, as are community volunteers from the business and professional community. They evaluate student performances and give students one-on-one feedback. Information from the student performances and the feedback students received on them is uploaded into the student's electronic portfolio, where he or she uses it to carry out more complex reflection and self-assessment across courses. Faculty and educational researchers use data to identify patterns in aggregate learning, and to validate the assessment techniques.

Social Interaction or Teamwork. The three assessments administered externally to courses that it is useful to discuss here supply information at the beginning, developing, and more advanced levels of student programs. In semester one, all entering students prepare for and complete an assessment on basic social interaction or teamwork in the Assessment Center, which deals with skills for the kind of task-oriented group work students will be using throughout their future Alverno coursework, employing other models as well.

In this performance assessment, students carry out a simulated candidate selection process, and so review information about the position and various applicants. They come together for a meeting done in fishbowl style, observed live by assessors who record behaviors. From the point of view of learning to integrate and apply, this assessment requires students to make sense of the perspectives of others in the meeting, explain their own views for why they would advocate for a particular candidate, and recognize the connection between their ideas and the realities of a decision. After the meeting is concluded, they carry out a self-assessment using behavioral criteria, thus working to establish the sort of metacognitive capacity necessary for using developing abilities as metacognitive strategies. In the feedback session, the assessor and student compare and discuss their behavioral observations, with the assessor responsible for the final judgment of success or failure.

Midprogram Assessment of General Education. Next, around the end of their second year, all students, including those who have transferred to Alverno from other institutions, take a midprogram assessment. In the current instrument—which changes depending on the curricular issue faculty are currently dealing with—they demonstrate scientific reasoning, quantitative literacy, analysis, valuing in decision making, and problem solving at selected levels of performance. They complete part one on their own by examining their drinking water habits through analysis and computation. They complete a self-assessment of strengths and weaknesses in their performance in prior coursework (at Alverno or elsewhere) and review faculty feedback and their own self-assessments on the developing abilities they are to demonstrate.

In part two, administered in the Assessment Center, they individually create a research question and hypothesis and test it using data provided—for example, on the chemical composition of bottled versus tap water—and then use the results to comment on their own values and decisions, as well as the cultural and pollution issues involved in the sharp increase in bottled-water consumption. They complete a self-assessment and receive feedback from a trained, cross-disciplinary assessor, who discusses their performance in relation to criteria met and unmet, with the assessor responsible for the final judgment. To succeed on this assessment, students need to draw explicitly on materials dealt with in a range of prerequisite courses in the natural sciences, behavioral sciences, and humanities. Further, they have to show they can use those concepts and capacities to discuss a contemporary problem in the community that directly affects their lives as citizens.

Effective Citizenship and Developing a Global Perspective. The third example of an assessment administered external to courses occurs at the junior-senior level, for judging advanced ability levels of effective citizenship and developing a global perspective. Students have completed general education courses on a local issue analyzed in its global context, and examined how citizens and governments address it, through the work of government agencies, NGOs, and other vehicles. Recent course themes have included water, cross-cultural changes in gender roles, terrorism, indigenous peoples, and power and prejudice. In this summative assessment, students participate in a simulated meeting of a team responsible for allocating $10 million in grants for NGO projects from around the world. Each student advocates for a particular NGO's project and must help the team come to consensus about the total allocations to the various NGOs. The group's larger task is to develop a set of shared criteria for making funding decisions. From their required courses they are in principle familiar with thinking globally and locally, and with disciplinary concepts and data that can be used to shed light on global problems. However, in the formal assessment itself they address a problem and analyze NGOs they specifically did not work on in their courses. Thus the assessment emphasizes adapting and transferring what they learned earlier to new, unscripted situations. The assessment is also an on-demand, complex performance of sophisticated levels of analysis, social interaction or teamwork, and judgment.

In sum, Alverno students demonstrate integrative and applied learning in courses and in a series of required assessments administered by an Assessment Center that places increasingly more complex demands for transferring their learning across courses and over time. For all of the assessments illustrated here, students upload assessment and self-assessment materials to Alverno's campuswide Diagnostic Digital Portfolio (DDP). Assessors also upload their feedback and evaluations of student work. This information is then used by students to create a developmental picture of their own learning, by faculty searching for patterns in student learning, and by educational researchers synthesizing it for program evaluation (see Cambridge, 2010, for a broader discussion of electronic portfolios).

Capstone Assessments in the Major Field. Assessing integrative and applied learning within disciplines and professions is accomplished through capstone courses and assessments, especially for observing developing abilities in practice settings. To forge a more institutional portrait of student work within these distinct territories, faculty have established opportunities to discuss ongoing, systematic conversations about students' performances in a way that can help departments share observations and improve practices. Capstone assessments are a relatively common strategy on many campuses. On ours, it shows up in the agendas of particular campus teams working closely on assessment issues, and also more broadly in our faculty development program.

Conclusions

Review Actual Student Performances from Different Points in Programs. By reviewing beginning, intermediate, and advanced examples of students' integration, application, and transfer at different points in the program, faculty are likely to expand their own educational theory and frameworks. In addition, because the process of integrating always involves putting past learning to work in a particular situation, examining learning at various points in the program allows us to see whether students can "get it all together" and "bring everything together in a situation that is unfamiliar."

Evaluate Performance Assessment Designs and Relationships Across Curricula. To uncover whether students are developing integrative and applied capacities that transfer learning to unfamiliar and unimagined settings requires us to place students in situations that elicit complex thinking and connect that thinking to acting in the setting. Assessment designs focus on reflective performances: simulations and projects requiring application of both capabilities and ideas, each at similar levels of complexity. Students who are learning how to perform in these settings benefit from the coherent experiences of a curriculum that makes such connections explicit, early and often. Assessments and curricula that signal coherence or alignment are especially beneficial for students in general education programs.

Curriculum-Embedded Assessments and Rubrics. When educators lament about students' weak capacity to integrate and apply, they often point fingers at both course assignments that do not demand higher-order thinking and at academic programs that reveal a lack of opportunities for students to demonstrate their developing abilities in situations where they have not initially learned them. We acknowledge that keeping coherence and alignment at the forefront is an ongoing challenge when faculty members are constantly modifying course assessments. Thus we recommend assessments that students complete to demonstrate integrative and applied learning with transfer across courses and over time, and with subsequent opportunities for reflection and self-assessment on performance in the curriculum and internships. However, without faculty who organize learning experiences for students to use broad college learning outcomes, such as learned abilities taught and assessed in the context of the disciplines, students are less likely to develop metacognitive strategies as frameworks for performing effectively, and sustain their learning through reflection and self-assessment. Those students who demonstrate such integrative and applied learning will more likely be effective in their volunteer roles in campus life and the local community, and their learning will more likely last well beyond college.

References

Alverno College Faculty. *Student Assessment-as-Learning at Alverno College.* Milwaukee, Wis.: Alverno College Institute, 1979/1994. (Original work published 1979, revised 1985 and 1994.)

Alverno College Faculty. *Self Assessment at Alverno College* (G. Loacker, ed.). Milwaukee, Wis.: Alverno College Institute, 2000.

American Association of Colleges and Universities (AACU). "Valid Assessment of Learning in Undergraduate Education (VALUE) Rubrics." 2009a. Retrieved Aug. 15, 2010, from http://www.aacu.org/value/rubrics/index.cfm.

American Association of Colleges and Universities (AACU). "VALUE: Valid Assessment of Learning in Undergraduate Education. "2009b. Retrieved Jan. 26, 2011, from http://aacu.org/value/.

Anastasi, A. "Abilities and the Measurement of Achievement." In W. B. Schrader (ed.), *Measuring Achievement: Progress over a Decade*. New Directions for Testing and Measurement, no. 5, , 1980.

Bierman, S., Ciner, E., Lauer-Glebov, J., Rutz, C., and Savina, M. "Integrative Learning: Coherence out of Chaos." *Peer Review*, Summer/Fall 2005, 18–20.

Bransford, J. D., Brown, A. L., and Cocking, R. R. (eds.). *How People Learn: Brain, Mind, Experience, and School* (expanded ed.). Washington, D.C.: National Academy Press, 2000.

Cambridge, D. *Eportfolios for Lifelong Learning and Assessment*. San Francisco: Jossey-Bass, 2010.

Chickering, A. W., with Mentkowski, M. "Assessing Ineffable Outcomes." In A. W. Chickering, J. C. Dalton, and L. Stamm, *Encouraging Authenticity and Spirituality in Higher Education*. San Francisco: Jossey-Bass, 2006.

Crain, C., and Rogers, G. (eds.). *Advancing Student Learning Outcomes in Community and Technical Colleges*. Milwaukee, Wis.: Alverno College Institute, 2010.

Darling-Hammond, L. "What Kind of Change Can We Believe In? Toward an Equitable System of Good Schools." Paper presented at the annual meeting of the American Educational Research Association, Denver, May 2, 2010.

Diez, M. E., Athanasiou, N., and Pointer Mace. D. "Expeditionary Learning: The Alverno College Teacher Education Model." *Change*, 2010, 42(6), 18–24.

Eraut, M. *Developing Professional Knowledge and Competence*. London: Falmer Press, 1994.

Feltovich, P. J., Prietula, M. J., and Ericsson, K. A. "Studies of Expertise from Psychological Perspectives." In K. A. Ericsson, N. Charness, P. J. Feltovich, and R. R. Hoffman (eds.), *The Cambridge Handbook of Expertise and Expert Performance*. Cambridge, UK: Cambridge University Press, 2006.

Guarasci, R., and Lieberman, T. "Sustaining Transformation: Resiliency in Hard Times." *Change*, 2009, 4(6), 24–31.

Holyoak, K. "Symbolic Connectionism: Toward Third-Generation Theories of Expertise." In K. A. Ericsson and J. Smith (eds.), *Toward a General Theory of Expertise: Prospects and Limits*. Cambridge, UK: Cambridge University Press, 1991.

Huber, M. T., and Hutchings, P. *Integrative Learning: Mapping the Terrain*. Washington, D.C.: Association of American Colleges and Universities, 2004. Retrieved Aug. 15, 2010, from http://www.lagcc.cuny.edu/CTL/conference05/pdf/Mapping_Terrain.pdf.

Kolb, D. A. *The Learning Style Inventory: Technical manual*. Boston: McBer, 1976.

Levi, A. J., and Stevens. D. D. "Assessment of the Academy, for the Academy, by the Academy." In T. L. Rhodes (ed.), *Assessing Outcomes and Improving Achievement: Tips and Tools for Using Rubrics*. Washington, D.C.: American Association of Higher Education, 2010.

Loacker, G., and Mentkowski, M. "Creating a Culture Where Assessment Improves Learning." In T. W. Banta and Associates, *Making a Difference: Outcomes of a Decade of Assessment in Higher Education*, 5–24. San Francisco: Jossey-Bass, 1993.

Loacker, G., and Riordan. T. "Collaborative and Systemic Assessment of Student Learning: From Principles to Practice." In G. Joughin (ed.), *Assessment, Learning and Judgement in Higher Education*. New York: Springer Science+Business Media B.V., 2009.

Loacker, G., and Rogers. G. *Assessment at Alverno College: Student, Program, Institutional.* Milwaukee, Wis.: Alverno College Institute, 2005.

Lobato, J. "How Design Experiments Can Inform a Rethinking of Transfer and Vice Versa." *Educational Researcher,* 2003, *32*(1), 17–20.

Mentkowski, M. "Accessible and Adaptable Elements of Alverno Student Assessment-as-Learning: Strategies and Challenges for Peer Review." In C. Bryan and K. Clegg (eds.), *Innovative Assessment in Higher Education.* London: Taylor and Francis, 2006.

Mentkowski, M. "Integrative and Applied Learning: What Do We Mean? How Do We Know? Why Do We Care?" Paper presented at the American Association of Colleges and Universities Conference, Integrative Learning: Addressing the Complexities, Atlanta, Oct. 23, 2009.

Mentkowski, M., and Associates. *Learning That Lasts: Integrating Learning, Development, and Performance in College and Beyond.* San Francisco: Jossey-Bass, 2000.

Mentkowski, M., and Doherty, A. "Abilities That Last a Lifetime: Outcomes of the Alverno Experience." *AAHE Bulletin,* 1984, *36*(6), 5–6, 11–14.

Mentkowski, M., and Loacker, G. "Assessing and Validating the Outcomes of College." In P. T. Ewell (ed.), *Assessing Educational Outcomes.* New Directions for Institutional Research, no. 47. San Francisco: Jossey-Bass, 1985.

Rhodes, T. L. (ed.). *Assessing Outcomes and Improving Achievement: Tips and Tools for Using Rubrics.* Washington, D.C.: American Association of Colleges and Universities, 2010.

Riordan, T., and Sharkey, S. "Hand in Hand: The Role of Culture, Faculty Identity, and Mission in Sustaining General Education Reform." In R. Barnett and S. Gano-Phillips (eds.), *A Process Approach to General Education Reform: Transforming Institutional Culture in Higher* Education. Madison, Wis.: Atwood, 2010.

Rogers, G. "Measurement and Judgment in Curriculum Assessment Systems." *Assessment Update,* 1994, *6*(1), 6–7.

Rogers, G., and Mentkowski, M. "Abilities That Distinguish the Effectiveness of Five-Year Alumna Performance Across Work, Family, and Civic Roles: A Higher Education Validation." *Higher Education Research and Development,* 2004, *23*(3), 347–374.

Rogers, G., Mentkowski, M., and Reisetter Hart, J. "Adult Holistic Development and Multidimensional Performance." In C. Hoare (ed.), *Handbook of Adult Development and Learning.* New York: Oxford University Press, 2006.

Schneider, C. G. "From the President." *Peer Review,* 2008, *10*(4), 3.

Schön, D. A. *Educating the Reflective Practitioner: Toward a New Design for Teaching and Learning in the Professions.* San Francisco: Jossey-Bass, 1987.

Sternberg, R. J. "Abilities Are Forms of Developing Expertise." *Educational Researcher,* 1998, *27*(3), 11–20.

Student Learning Initiative. *Student Learning: A Central Focus for Institutions of Higher Education* (A. Doherty, T. Riordan, and J. Roth, eds.). Milwaukee, Wis.: Alverno College Institute, 2002.

MARCIA MENTKOWSKI *is senior scholar for educational research, professor of psychology, and founding director emerita of the Educational Research and Evaluation Department at Alverno College. She is the lead author of* Learning That Lasts: Integrating Learning, Development, and Performance in College and Beyond, *a series of studies on integrative and applied learning.*

STEPHEN SHARKEY *is professor of sociology and dean of the School of Arts and Sciences at Alverno College. He is an associate author of* Learning That Lasts.

*This chapter examines how changes to faculty members' roles,
changes to students' expectations for higher education, and
increasing demand for accountability affect general education
assessment practices. An agenda for future research on general
education assessment is proposed.*

9

Future Directions for Assessing
Complex General Education Student
Learning Outcomes

Jeremy D. Penn

In 1933–34, a few years before the landmark study on student achievement
by Learned and Wood (1938), the total enrollment of students in colleges,
universities, junior colleges, teachers colleges, and normal schools was
around 1.06 million (Committee Y of the American Association of University Professors, 1937) out of a U.S. population of about 126.5 million (U.S.
Census Bureau, 2002), or about 0.8 percent. In 2008, the total projected fall
enrollment in postsecondary, degree-granting institutions was over 18 million (National Center for Education Statistics, 2009) out of a U.S. population of 304 million (U.S. Census Bureau, 2008), or about 6 percent. The
dramatic change in enrollment and participation in higher education is only
one of many transformations that continue to dramatically affect every
aspect of postsecondary education. This chapter examines three major
trends in postsecondary education, related to faculty members' roles, students' changing expectations for postsecondary education, and increasing
demands for access, affordability, and accountability. It also discusses how
they have an impact on assessment of general education student learning
outcomes. The chapter closes by proposing an agenda for future research.

Casualization of Faculty Work

In 1980, 62 percent of full-time faculty members at four-year institutions
classified as baccalaureate or higher according to the Carnegie Classification were tenured (IPEDS, 2010). In 1992, this percentage decreased

New Directions for Institutional Research, no. 149, Spring 2011 © Wiley Periodicals, Inc.
Published online in Wiley Online Library (wileyonlinelibrary.com) • DOI: 10.1002/ir.384

slightly to 61 percent, and an additional 25 percent of faculty members were on the tenure track (IPEDS, 2010). However, by 2008 the proportion of full-time tenured faculty members had decreased to 45 percent, and only 20 percent were on the tenure track, leaving a large number of full-time faculty members off it (IPEDS, 2010).

This trend, reflecting a move away from use of tenured and tenure-track faculty members toward increased use of nontenure-track faculty members and part-time, contingent instructors, is part of what has been called the "casualization" of work in higher education (see Berry, 2005; Percy and Beaumont, 2008). Casual jobs are those that "attract an hourly rate of pay but very few of the other rights and benefits, such as the right to notice, the right to severance pay, and most forms of paid leave" (May, Campbell, and Burgess, 2005). The casualization of faculty work reflects changes not only to the granting of tenure and tenure-track status but also to the relationship between institutions and faculty members, substantially affecting faculty members' roles and responsibilities.

Students' Changing Approaches to Higher Education and the Rise of the McUniversity

In the late 1960s, a survey found more than 80 percent of college students endorsed "developing a meaningful philosophy of life" as an essential or very important reason for attending college, while only 45 percent endorsed "being well off financially." By the late 1980s, these two goals had switched places, with "being well off financially" the top goal and "developing a meaningful philosophy of life" dropping to sixth place (Astin, 1998). Another important indicator of the striking changes to how students approach higher education is the large percentage who attend more than one institution before graduating. Fifty-nine percent of first-time bachelor's degree recipients in 1999–2000 attended more than one institution (Peter and Forrest Cataldi, 2005) as students engaged in what has been called "swirling" and "double-dipping" (McCormick, 2003). Higher education is now only one of many things that occupy students' time during the day, with 68 percent of all college students working for pay during the academic year (Pike, Kuh, and Massa-McKinley, 2008).

These elements taken together have been called the rise of the McUniversity (Ritzer, 1996), which entails viewing students as consumers and responding to their "new means of consumption" (Baudrillard, 1970; cited in Ritzer, 1996, p. 185). Although there are many issues that arise when institutions begin viewing students as consumers (see Olshavsky and Spreng, 1995), many students and parents already take this approach to their education. These students want the McUniversity to provide "simple procedures, good service, quality courses, and low costs" (Levine, 1993), resulting in increasing pressure for "serious reconsideration of our assumptions of how, when, and where instruction (and education more broadly) can be delivered and learning promoted" (Pascarella and Terenzini, 1998, pp. 161–162).

Increasing Demand for Access, Affordability, and Accountability

Access, affordability, and accountability have become focal points for reform in higher education (see Webber and Boehmer, 2008; U.S. Department of Education, 2006). Access to higher education is "unduly limited by the complex interplay of inadequate preparation, lack of information about college opportunities, and persistent financial barriers" (U.S. Department of Education, 2006, p. 1) and is particularly problematic for low-income groups and some racial and ethnic minorities. Affordability, closely linked with access (Adelman, 2007), is becoming increasingly difficult for many students as the cost of college "has significantly outpaced the growth of family incomes" (Middle Class Task Force, 2009). Accountability is viewed as a mechanism to "ensure that colleges succeed in educating students" and as a way to answer "basic questions" on the cost of college and on "which institutions do a better job than others not only of graduating students but of teaching them what they need to learn" (U.S. Department of Education, 2006, p. x). The drive for increased access, affordability, and accountability has an impact on our institutions' educational missions and how we seek to carry them out.

Together, the casualization of faculty work, changes in how students approach higher education, and the push for access, affordability, and accountability challenge our traditional general education assessment processes and highlight four future directions for assessment of general education: (1) innovation in assessment tools, methods, and uses; (2) development of consortia of institutions to collaborate on general education assessment; (3) movement from the institution to the student as the unit of analysis; and (4) using assessment to inform our understanding of the credit hour.

Future Directions for Assessment of General Education

Innovation in Assessment Tools, Methods, and Uses. General education outcomes are continuing to move away from a grouping of discipline-based, cafeteria-style courses toward an emphasis on transferable, complex, cross-discipline student learning outcomes. As discussed in the earlier chapters in this volume, one result of this development is creation of innovative assessment tools designed to gather evidence of student achievement of these complex outcomes. Methods and processes for using these new assessment tools must also be created to reflect new educational practices and the new ways in which students interact with multiple

NEW DIRECTIONS FOR INSTITUTIONAL RESEARCH • DOI: 10.1002/ir

institutions. These assessment methods must be simple, straightforward, and efficient to permit use by a diverse, and increasingly nontenure-track, faculty with a mobile student body.

Assessment of general education will be used in a variety of ways and for many purposes. As faculty members' and students' roles evolve and change, assessment of general education will be even more critical in establishing expectations for student achievement of the general education outcomes and communicating those outcomes with faculty members, students, external stakeholders, accreditors, and the general public. Data from assessment of general education will continue to be used to improve and revise the general education program while simultaneously serving accountability demands.

Developing Consortia of Institutions to Jointly Assess General Education Learning Outcomes. As a result of the large number of students enrolling at multiple institutions or transferring between institutions, most degree programs and general education programs are now cross-institutional. Assessment of general education programs has traditionally either ignored this reality or focused only on the smaller group of traditional students. Consortia of institutions need to be developed in order to integrate assessment across institutions, so users of assessment results have a more complete picture of the relationship between educational programs and student achievement.

These new consortia would be based on core groups of shared students and would work across Carnegie classification status to achieve both horizontal and vertical integration, ideally growing to also include K–12 schools. Each consortium should work to build a shared set of expectations for student achievement in general education, create cross-institutional curricula that address these expectations, and establish a systematic process for gathering assessment data on students' achievement of these expectations. The Tuning model from the Bologna process (see Adelman, 2008; Lumina Foundation, 2010) may be one such approach.

Moving from the Institution to the Student as the Unit of Analysis. One primary purpose for implementing assessment of general education is to draw inferences about curricula, co-curricular experiences, and teaching practices so as to develop improvement strategies. A common method being used to draw such inferences, and a widespread component of current accountability initiatives, is to administer a common test or rubric for the purpose of comparing student achievement at the institutional level. This method is appealing because it can be used to rank-order institutions and could reveal successful institutional practices that lead to increased student achievement. However, institutional-level analyses are problematic because they focus on the small portion of the variance in student achievement between institutions, while ignoring the large variance in student achievement within an institution (see Braun, Jenkins, and Grigg, 2006). If the institution is used as the unit of analysis,

NEW DIRECTIONS FOR INSTITUTIONAL RESEARCH • DOI: 10.1002/ir

a considerable amount of information about differences in student achievement is lost, hampering our ability to draw useful and meaningful inferences about our curricula, co-curricular experiences, and teaching practices.

If we focus on the student as the unit of analysis, our assessment reports read as a multiple case study that carefully examines each student's skills and abilities relative to our expectations for learning and seeks to understand how the educational opportunities offered to each student could be enhanced to address needed improvements. A student-focused report allows focus on the curricular, teaching, and co-curricular activities that were experienced, and it encourages consideration of what could have been offered that would have better enabled the student to achieve the general education student learning outcomes. Instead of focusing solely on quantitative methodology, assessment practice should also embrace qualitative or mixed-methods research approaches that can better reveal individual students' experiences in our programs and institutions.

Using Assessment to Inform Our Understanding of the Credit Hour. The debate over the value of a credit hour and whether or not it is a suitable proxy for learning is at least twenty-five years old (see Study Group on the Conditions of Excellence in American Higher Education, 1984). Learned and Wood (1938) explored how graduating classes would look if degrees were granted on the basis of achievement (for example, the top 20 percent of examinees on a set of comprehensive examinations) instead of on accumulated credit hours. They found 15 percent of students in this new group were freshmen, 19 percent were sophomores, 21 percent were juniors, and 28 percent were seniors—underscoring the differences between credit hours and assessment.

As institutions continue to move general education programs toward a learning outcomes approach and away from cafeteria-style credit hour accumulation, assessment of general education must mature so it can inform and enhance our understanding of the credit hour. Although credit hours will still be an important component, institutions may find it more desirable to express general education requirements in terms of expected student achievement than the expected number of earned credit hours. General education programs of this nature could be designed so that most students achieve the desired learning in twenty-five to forty-five credit hours, although it may take fewer or more credits for some students. Credit hours and assessment work together throughout the general education program to inform student progress, certify every student's achievement of the general education student learning outcomes, and provide information for accountability and improvement of the general education program. Within established consortia of institutions, students' demonstrations of achievement of the general education outcomes, together with the credit hour, become the general education credential.

Future Research

The authors of the previous chapters in this volume have suggested many avenues for future research. Three additional lines of research should be added to the list. First, as part of an agenda being tackled by the National Institute for Learning Outcomes Assessment (NILOA), additional research is needed to enhance our understanding of how to best use assessment data "internally to inform and strengthen undergraduate education, and externally to communicate with policy makers, families and other stakeholders" (NILOA, 2010, para. 2). Specifically in general education, research is needed to inform policy, curricular, and pedagogical innovations that should be implemented to improve student achievement in particular general education student learning outcomes. Clear guidance on innovations that improve student achievement on the general education learning outcomes would go a long way toward enhancing use of assessment data.

Second, research is needed to better understand the relationship between general education student learning outcomes and the disciplines. Many scholars have recommended approaching general education learning outcomes across disciplines (see Audet and Jordan, 2005, on inquiry across the curriculum; Branche, Mullennix, and Cohn, 2007, on diversity across the curriculum; Behrens and Rosen, 1997, on writing and reading across the curriculum; and the National Leadership Council for Liberal Education and America's Promise, 2007). In this approach, the disciplines are the vehicles through which the general education outcomes are achieved. However, other scholars (see Beyer, Gillmore, and Fisher, 2007; Eljamal and others, 1998) have suggested the transfer of general skills between disciplines is limited and that they are specific to the discipline. More research is needed to better understand the transfer of general education student learning outcomes between disciplines and how the disciplines can best contribute to their achievement.

Finally, most individuals working in assessment in higher education have at one time or another been challenged to produce clear evidence that assessment improves student learning. Without this evidence, as the argument goes, assessment should be avoided because it is nothing more than an administrative demand to "make a pig fatter by weighing it." Although research in this area may be interesting, it is unnecessary, as argued in Chapter One, because we should be engaging in assessment as part of our responsibility as faculty members to ensure our educational practices are achieving the goals we set for our students.

The research agenda that gets lost in the quest for proof of the value of assessment in improving student learning is the question of how assessment data inform decision-making processes. A central tenet of the assessment philosophy is that including evidence on student achievement as an element in the decision-making process leads to better decisions. This stance assumes decision makers employ reason as the central decision-making process, using, as Thomas Jefferson put it, "[God-bestowed] reason . . . as the umpire of truth" (1903, p. 197). Use of assessment data is thought to remove the emotional element from the decision-making process and ensure high-quality, well-reasoned decisions. Lehrer (2009) suggested that decisions are not generally made only for rational reasons, and also that without an emotional component to the decision-making process it is "impossible to make decent decisions" (p. 18), the function of emotion being to support reasoned decisions. More research is needed in the assessment field to better understand these decision-making processes—to offer guidance on proper use of assessment evidence, to compare the differences in decision-making processes that are made with and without assessment evidence, and to better understand the balance between presentation of objective assessment data and more personal narratives designed to activate the emotional component of decision makers' minds. Research on how we get the most out of our investment in assessment is important, but I suspect it will be intimately related to the quality of the decisions we make in our use of assessment data.

Conclusion

In this volume, the authors have made a case for assessment of general education; provided a structure and model called TAIM for developing and improving the assessment process; presented guidance on the current research on definitions, methodology, and practices for assessing a core set of general education student learning outcomes; and suggested directions for future research and exploration. Assessment of complex general education student learning outcomes is our responsibility as faculty members; it offers tremendous potential to inform, transform, and improve our general education programs.

References

Adelman, C. "Do We Really Have a College Access Problem?" *Change*, 2007, *39*(4), 48–51.

Adelman, C. *The Bologna Club: What U.S. Higher Education Can Learn from a Decade of European Reconstruction.* Washington, D.C.: Institute for Higher Education Policy, 2008.

Astin, A. "The Changing American College Student: Thirty-Year Trends, 1966–1996." *Review of Higher Education*, 1998, *21*(2), 115–135.

Audet, R. H., and Jordan, L. K. (eds.). *Integrating Inquiry Across the Curriculum.* Thousand Oaks, Calif.: Corwin, 2005.

Behrens, L., and Rosen, L. J. *Writing and Reading Across the Curriculum.* New York: Longman, 1997.

Berry, J. *Reclaiming the Ivory Tower: Organizing Adjuncts to Change Higher Education.* New York: Monthly Review, 2005.

Beyer, C. H., Gillmore, G. M., and Fisher, A. T. *Inside the Undergraduate Experience: The University of Washington's Study of Undergraduate Learning.* Bolton, Mass.: Anker, 2007.

Branche, J., Mullennix, J., and Cohn, E. R. *Diversity Across the Curriculum: A Guide for Faculty in Higher Education.* Bolton, Mass.: Anker, 2007.

Braun, H., Jenkins, F., and Grigg, W. *Comparing Private Schools and Public Schools Using Hierarchical Linear Modeling.* U.S. Department of Education, National Center for Education Statistics, Institute of Education Sciences. Washington, D.C.: U.S. Government Printing Office, 2006. (NCES 2006-461)

Committee Y of the American Association of University Professors. *Depression, Recovery and Higher Education.* New York: McGraw-Hill, 1937.

Eljamal, M. B., Sharp, S., Stark, J. S., Arnold, G. L., and Lowther, M. A. "Listening for Disciplinary Differences in Faculty Goals for Effective Thinking." *Journal of General Education,* 1998, 47(2), 117–147.

IPEDS. "IPEDS Data Center," 2010. U.S. Department of Education, Institute of Education Sciences, National Center for Education Statistics. Retrieved Mar. 23, 2010, from http://nces.ed.gov/ipeds/datacenter/Default.aspx.

Jefferson, T. "To Miles King, September 26, 1814." In A. A. Lipscomb and A. E. Bergth (eds.). *The Writings of Thomas Jefferson* (vol. 14). Washington, D.C.: The Thomas Jefferson Memorial Association, 1903.

Learned, W. S., and Wood, B. D. *The Student and His Knowledge.* New York: Carnegie Foundation for the Advancement of Teaching, 1938.

Lehrer, J. *How We Decide.* Boston: Houghton Mifflin Harcourt, 2009.

Levine, A. "Student Expectations of College." *Change,* 1993, 25(5), 4.

Lumina Foundation. "Tuning USA." Retrieved June 21, 2010, from http://www.luminafoundation.org/our_work/tuning/.

May, R., Campbell, I., and Burgess, J. "The Rise and Rise of Casual Work in Australia: Who Benefits, Who Loses?" Paper presented at Sydney University, June 20, 2005.

McCormick, A. "Swirling and Double-Dipping: New Patterns of Student Attendance and Their Implications for Higher Education." In *Changing Student Attendance Patterns: Challenges for Practice and Policy.* (Special Issue.) New Directions for Higher Education, no. 121, 2003, 13–24.

Middle Class Task Force, Staff Report. "Financing the Dream: Securing College Affordability for the Middle Class." 2009. Retrieved May 18, 2010, from http://www.whitehouse.gov/assets/documents/staff_report_college_affordability1.pdf.

National Center for Education Statistics. "Fast Facts, 2009." Retrieved Apr. 21, 2010, from http://nces.ed.gov/fastfacts/display.asp?id=98.

National Institute for Learning Outcomes Assessment (NILOA). "National Institute for Learning Outcomes Assessment: Our Mission and Vision." 2010. Retrieved May 13, 2010, from http://www.learningoutcomeassessment.org/AboutUs.html.

National Leadership Council for Liberal Education and America's Promise. "College Learning for the New Global Century: A Report from the National Leadership Council for Liberal Education and America's Promise." 2007. Retrieved Sept. 17, 2009, from http://www.aacu.org/leap/documents/GlobalCentury_final.pdf.

Olshavsky, R. W., and Spreng, R. A. "Consumer Satisfaction and Students: Some Pitfalls of Being Customer Driven." *Journal of Consumer Satisfaction, Dissatisfaction, and Complaining Behavior,* 1995, 8, 69–77.

Pascarella, E. T., and Terenzini, P. T. "Studying College Students in the 21st Century: Meeting New Challenges." *Review of Higher Education,* 1998, 21(2), 151–165.

Percy, A., and Beaumont, R. "The Casualisation of Teaching and the Subject of Risk." *Studies in Continuing Education,* 2008, 30(2), 145–157.

Peter, K., and Forrest Cataldi, E. *The Road Less Traveled? Students Who Enroll in Multiple Institutions.* U.S. Department of Education, National Center for Education Statistics. Washington, D.C.: U.S. Government Printing Office, 2005. (NCES 2005-157)

Pike, G. R., Kuh, G. D., & Massa-McKinley, R. C. "First-Year Students' Employment, Engagement, and Academic Achievement: Untangling the Relationship Between Work and Grades." *NASPA Journal*, 2008, *45*(4), 560–582.

Ritzer, G. "McUniversity in the Postmodern Consumer Society." *Quality in Higher Education*, 1996, *2*(3), 185–199.

Study Group on the Conditions of Excellence in American Higher Education. *Involvement in Learning: Realizing the Potential of American Higher Education*. Washington, D.C.: National Institute of Education, 1984.

U.S. Census Bureau. "Population: 1900 to 2002." No. HS-1. 2002. Retrieved May 17, 2010, from http://www.census.gov/statab/hist/HS-01.pdf.

U.S. Census Bureau. "Population estimates, 2008." Retrieved May 17, 2010, from http://www.census.gov/popest/states/NST-ann-est2008.html.

U.S. Department of Education. *A Test of Leadership: Charting the Future of U.S. Higher Education*. Washington, D.C.: U.S. Department of Education, 2006.

Webber, K. L., and Boehmer, R. G. "The Balancing Act: Accountability, Affordability, and Access in American Higher Education." In *International Perspectives on Accountability, Affordability, and Access to Postsecondary Education*. (Special Issue.) New Directions for Institutional Research, no. S2, 2008, 79–91.

JEREMY D. PENN *is the director of assessment and testing and an adjunct faculty member in the School of Educational Studies at Oklahoma State University.*

NEW DIRECTIONS FOR INSTITUTIONAL RESEARCH • DOI: 10.1002/ir

INDEX

119

OTHER TITLES AVAILABLE IN THE
NEW DIRECTIONS FOR INSTITUTIONAL RESEARCH SERIES
Robert K. Toutkoushian, Editor-in-Chief

IR 148　**Students of Color in STEM**
Shaun R. Harper, Christopher B. Newman
Why are some racial minorities so underrepresented as degree candidates in
science, technology, engineering, and mathematics (STEM)? Why are they
so underprepared for college-level math and science courses? Why are their
grades and other achievement indicators disproportionately lower than their
white counterparts? Why do so many of them change their majors to non-
STEM fields? And why do so few pursue graduate degrees in STEM? These
five questions are continuously recycled in the study of students of color in
STEM. Offered in this volume of *New Directions for Institutional Research* are
new research ideas and frameworks that have emerged from recent studies
of minorities in STEM fields across a wide array of institution types: large
research universities, community colleges, minority-serving institutions,
and others. The chapter authors counterbalance examinations of student
underperformance and racial disparities in STEM with insights into the
study of factors that enable minority student success.
ISBN: 978-1-1180-1402-8

IR 147　**System Offices for Community College Institutional Research**
Willard C. Hom
This volume of *New Directions for Institutional Research* examines a
professional niche that tends to operate with a low profile while playing
a major role in state policies—the system office for community college
institutional research. As states, regions, and the federal government seek
ways to evaluate and improve the performance of community colleges,
this office has grown in importance. The chapter authors, all institutional
researchers in this area, draw a timely state-of-the-niche portrait by showing
how this office varies across states, how it varies from other institutional
research offices within states, and the implications its history and prospects
have for the future. This volume will be particularly useful for those who
deal with higher education policy at the state, regional, or federal level;
on-campus institutional researchers; and individuals who currently work in
or with these system offices.
ISBN: 978-04709-39543

IR 146　**Institutional Research and Homeland Security**
Nicolas A. Valcik
Although homeland security has captured the public's attention in recent
years, higher education institutions have had to contend with emergency
situations and security issues long before 9/11 occurred. Well known
incidents such as the Unabomber attacks and decades of sporadic school
shootings brought violence to college campuses long before the Department
of Homeland Security was established. Despite these past security issues and
the passage of the PATRIOT Act, very little research has been performed on
homeland security issues and higher education institutions. This volume
of *New Directions for Institutional Research* examines how new federal
regulations impact institutional research and higher education institutions.
This volume also addresses key issues such as right-to-privacy regulations,
criminal background checks, the Student and Exchange Visitor Information

System (SEVIS), information technology security, the use of geographic information systems as a research tool, hazardous materials (HAZMAT) management, and the impact of natural disasters and manmade threats on applications and enrollment.
ISBN: 978-04709-03148

IR 145   **Diversity and Educational Benefits**
Serge Herzog
Campus climate studies and research on the impact of diversity in higher education abound. On closer examination, however, the corpus of findings on the role of diversity and how diversity is captured with campus climate surveys reveals both conceptual and methodological limitations. This volume of *New Directions for Institutional Research* addresses these limitations with the inclusion of studies by institutional research (IR) practitioners who make use of data that furnish new insights into the relationships among student diversity, student perception of campus climate, and student sociodemographic background—and how those relationships affect academic outcomes. Each chapter emphasizes how IR practitioners benefit from the conceptual and analytical approach laid out, and each chapter provides a framework to gauge the contribution of diversity to educational benefits. The findings revealed in this volume cast doubt on the benefits of student diversity purported in previous research. At a minimum, the influence of student diversity is neither linear nor unidirectional, but operates within a complex web of interrelated factors that shape the student experience.
ISBN: 978-04707-67276

IR 144   **Data-Driven Decision Making in Intercollegiate Athletics**
Jennifer Lee Hoffman, James Soto Antony, Daisy D. Alfaro
Data related to intercollegiate athletics are often a small part of campus financial and academic data reporting, but they generate significant interest at any institution that sponsors varsity sports. The demands for documentation, accountability, and data-driven decision making related to college athletics have grown increasingly sophisticated. These demands come from the press, campus decision makers, researchers, state and federal agencies, the National Collegiate Athletic Association, and the public. Despite the growth of data sources and the ease of access that information technology affords, gaps still exist between what we think we know about college athletics and supporting data. The challenge for institutional researchers is to continue developing consistent data sources that inform the policy and governance of college athletics. This volume of *New Directions for Institutional Research* introduces the reader to the primary and secondary sources of data on college athletics and their utility for decision making. The authors describe the existing landscape of data about student athletes and intercollegiate athletics and the measures that are still needed.
ISBN: 978-04706-08289

IR 143   **Imagining the Future of Institutional Research**
Christina Leimer
With the increasing demands placed on colleges and universities—requirements for continuous improvement, evidence-based decision making, and accountability—institutional research offices must do more than report and fill data requests. In the context of shrinking budgets, institutions must search for more efficient and effective ways of working, make decisions about which work will continue to be performed and how, and perhaps reorganize their existing programs, structures, and patterns. This too may demand more of institutional research. A decade ago, M. W. Peterson pro-posed in volume 104 of *New Directions for Institutional Research* that the future challenge for

institutional research would be not only to help institu-tions improve but to help facilitate their redesign and transformation. It appears that time has arrived. At most institutions, however, for institutional research to play such a substantive role, the field will need to redesign and transform itself. In this volume, the editor and authors take a proactive, strategic stance by imagining the future of institutional research and how to achieve it. ISBN: 978-04705-69269

IR 142   **Conducting Research on Asian Americans in Higher Education**
Samuel D. Museus
This volume of *New Directions for Institutional Research* moves beyond pervasive oversimplified and preconceived notions about Asian Americans in higher education and offers new directions in studying this population. The authors highlight the complexities inherent in the realities of Asian Americans in higher education. In addition to deconstructing common misconceptions that lead to the invisibility of Asian Americans in higher education research, they discuss methodological issues related to disaggre-gating data, assessing programmatic interventions, conducting campus climate research, engaging Asian American undergraduates in the research process, and using critical perspectives related to Asian Americans. They also discuss key challenges and future directions in research on this population. ISBN: 978-04705-29614

IR 141   **Using NSSE in Institutional Research**
Robert M. Gonyea, George D. Kuh
Student engagement is now part of the higher education lexicon in North America. This *New Directions for Institutional Research* volume explains the value and relevance of the construct, with an emphasis on how results from the National Survey of Student Engagement have been used for various purposes. Because process indicators are often used as proxy measures for institutional quality, the chapter authors discuss how student engagement data can help colleges and universities satisfy the demand for more evidence, accountability, and transparency of student and institutional performance. The widespread uses of student engagement results have helped to increase the visibility and importance of campus assessment efforts and of institutional researchers, who provide campus leaders with objective, trustworthy data about student and institutional performance. ISBN: 978-04704-99283

IR 140   **Using Financial and Personnel Data in a Changing World for Institutional Research**
Nicolas A. Valcik
This volume of *New Directions for Institutional Research* explores the ways in which financial and human resource data can be used in reporting and analysis. With public sources of revenue stagnating or declining and tuition costs increasing, the need for improved efficiencies in an institution's internal practices has become paramount. An institutional research department can use financial and human resource data to conduct analyses of institutional business practices to forecast costs and identify revenue generation. The chapter authors review the use of personnel, expenditure, and revenue data in the performance of institutional research from several perspectives: the role of organizational theory in data mining efforts, integration of various data sources for effective analyses, methodologies for more efficient faculty compensation benchmarking, the impact of state legislative decisions on revenue streams, and return on investment calculations. ISBN: 978-04704-68517

IR139   Conducting Institutional Research in Non-Campus-Based Settings
         Robert K. Toutkoushian, Tod R. Massa
         One aspect of the institutional research (IR) profession that has not
         been well documented is the many ways that this research is carried out
         beyond the confines of a traditional campus-based IR office. The purpose of
         this volume of *New Directions for Institutional Research* is to provide readers
         with insight into some of these alternatives and help expand understanding
         of the nature of institutional research. The chapters in this volume show
         how institutional research is being conducted by public university system
         offices, state higher education coordinating boards, institutional-affiliated
         research offices, and higher education consultants. Because these entities
         often do not have ready access to campus-specific data, they must be creative
         in finding ways to obtain data and information that enable them to provide
         a value-added function in the field. The chapter authors highlight ways in
         which these offices acquire and use information for institutional research.
         ISBN: 978-04704-12749

IR138   Legal Applications of Data for Institutional Research
         Andrew L. Luna
         This volume of *New Directions for Institutional Research* explores the seem-
         ingly incongruent forces of statistical reasoning and the law and sheds some
         light on how institutional researchers can use the two in a complementary
         manner to prevent a legal action or to help support the rebuttal of a prima
         facie case (i.e., one that at first glance presents sufficient evidence for the
         plaintiff to win the case). Until now, there has been little linkage between
         the disciplines of law and statistics. While the legal profession uses statistics
         to support an argument, interpretations of statistical outcomes may not
         follow scientific reasoning. Similarly, a great piece of statistical theory or a
         tried-and-true methodology among institutional research professionals may
         be thrown out of court if it fails to meet the rules of evidence or contradicts
         current legal standing. The information contained within this volume will
         benefit institutional research practitioners and contribute to a more frequent
         dialogue concerning the complexities of statistical science within the legal
         environment.
         ISBN: 978-04703-97619

IR137   Alternative Perspectives in Institutional Planning
         Terry T. Ishitani
         Institutional planning is coming to the fore in higher education as states,
         the federal government, and the public increasingly demand accountability.
         Institutional researchers, the data stewards for colleges and universities,
         are becoming involved in such strategic planning, supporting efforts to
         strengthen institutional efficiency and effectiveness in policymaking.
         Researchers find that locating, preparing, and presenting necessary data and
         information for planners is a challenging exercise. In this volume of *New
         Directions for Institutional Research*, administrators, consultants, researchers,
         and scholars provide unique, innovative approaches to that challenge. Some
         authors introduce program applications and statistical techniques; others
         share case studies. The variety of perspectives and depths of focus makes this
         a timely, useful guide for institutional researchers.
         ISBN: 978-04703-84534

NEW DIRECTIONS FOR INSTITUTIONAL RESEARCH
ORDER FORM SUBSCRIPTION AND SINGLE ISSUES

DISCOUNTED BACK ISSUES:

Use this form to receive 20% off all back issues of *New Directions for Institutional Research*.
All single issues priced at **$23.20** (normally $29.00)

TITLE	ISSUE NO.	ISBN

Call 888-378-2537 or see mailing instructions below. When calling, mention the promotional code JBNND to receive your discount. For a complete list of issues, please visit www.josseybass.com/go/ndir

SUBSCRIPTIONS: (1 YEAR, 4 ISSUES)

☐ New Order   ☐ Renewal

U.S.	☐ Individual: $100	☐ Institutional: $280
CANADA/MEXICO	☐ Individual: $100	☐ Institutional: $320
ALL OTHERS	☐ Individual: $124	☐ Institutional: $354

Call 888-378-2537 or see mailing and pricing instructions below.
Online subscriptions are available at www.onlinelibrary.wiley.com

ORDER TOTALS:

Issue / Subscription Amount: $ _____

Shipping Amount: $ _____
(for single issues only – subscription prices include shipping)

Total Amount: $ _____

SHIPPING CHARGES:
First Item $5.00
Each Add'l Item $3.00

(No sales tax for U.S. subscriptions. Canadian residents, add GST for subscription orders. Individual rate subscriptions must be paid by personal check or credit card. Individual rate subscriptions may not be resold as library copies.)

BILLING & SHIPPING INFORMATION:

☐ **PAYMENT ENCLOSED:** *(U.S. check or money order only. All payments must be in U.S. dollars.)*
☐ **CREDIT CARD:** ☐ VISA ☐ MC ☐ AMEX

Card number _____Exp. Date_____

Card Holder Name_____Card Issue # _____

Signature _____Day Phone_____

☐ **BILL ME:** *(U.S. institutional orders only. Purchase order required.)*

Purchase order # _____
Federal Tax ID 13559302 • GST 89102-8052

Name_____

Address_____

Phone_____ E-mail_____

Copy or detach page and send to: **John Wiley & Sons, PTSC, 5th Floor**
989 Market Street, San Francisco, CA 94103-1741

Order Form can also be faxed to: **888-481-2665**

PROMO JBNND